Flannelboard Classic Tales

Written and Adapted by
Doris Lynn Hicks

Patterns and Illustrates by
Sandy Weber Mahaffey

AMERICAN LIBRARY ASSOCIATION
Chicago and London
1997

Project manager: Joan A. Grygel

Photographs: Sandy Weber Mahaffey

Cover art: Richmond Jones

Text design: Dianne M. Rooney

Composition in Times and Futura Extrabold
using Xyvision by the dotted i.

Printed on 50-pound Victor Offset, a pH-neutral stock,
and bound in 10-point C1S cover stock by Victor
Graphics.

The paper used in this publication meets the minimum
requirements of American National Standard for
Information Sciences—Permanence of Paper for Printed
Library Materials, ANSI Z39.48-1992. ∞

Library of Congresss Cataloging-in-Publication Data

Hicks, Doris Lynn.
    Flannelboard classic tales / written and adapted by
Doris Lynn Hicks : patterns and illustrations by Sandy
Weber Mahaffey.
        p.   cm.
    ISBN 0-8389-0654-0
    1. Flannel boards.   2. Children's stories.
3. Storytelling.   I. Mahaffey, Sandy Weber, ill.
II. Title.
LB1043.62.H53   1997
371.3'35—dc20   96-43059

Printed in the United States of America

01 00 99 98 97   5 4 3 2 1

To Liza,
the librarian who taught me
about storytelling.
D.L.H.

To Courtney and Candace,
the two reasons I believe in "fairy tale"
love and "happily-ever-after" endings.
S.W.M.

Contents

Introduction

Classic Tales

For as long as anyone can remember, teachers and librarians have been presenting folktales to children. Some of the stories, such as the eighteen classic stories adapted in this book for flannelboard presentation, have survived in various oral and written forms for hundreds of years.

Folktales or fairy tales are entertaining stories with action-filled plots. Their characters seek to fill the basic human needs: food, shelter, love, even survival itself. The stories develop universal themes from the depths of human experience, such as overcoming fear, suffering ridicule, or achieving recognition. Although several folktales include noble rulers and supernatural creatures, the stories always feature protagonists who are not only common folk but also underdogs. It is little wonder that these stories appeal to children during their many years of being small and powerless in a world controlled by adults.

Cultures have passed along their values and customs to countless generations through their folktales. The art form of folktale/fairy tale is a part of every person's cultural heritage. W. H. Auden called the *Grimm's Fairy Tales* one of "the few indispensable, common-property books upon which Western culture can be founded." [1] Children who see and hear these stories will become adults who recognize literary and cultural allusions to the old tales' characters and events. Through exposure to these characters and plots children gain part of their cultural heritage and common knowledge, broaden their familiarity with other places, and deepen their understanding of diverse cultures. In our modern global community, children need to become acquainted not only with Rapunzel, the Gingerbread Man, and the Big Bad Wolf of western folktales but also with Coyote, Ananse, and other characters from the classic stories of non-European cultures.

Reading Aloud

Story telling with a flannelboard has value in the school and library program beyond that of being an enjoyable art form. One benefit is that this oral presentation of tales helps to build the child's vocabulary. Jim Trelease believes that "listening vocabulary is the reservoir of words that feeds the reading vocabulary pool." [2] Children learn new vocabulary in the meaningful context of the story, and the visual clues from the felt figures and context clues in the sentences help listeners figure out the meaning of the new words.

May Hill Arbuthnot addressed the educational value of fairy tales specifically when she wrote about four values of reading aloud to children. These were to develop listening comprehension skills needed in work and social relationships throughout life, expand reading interests, enjoy literature above the child's independent reading level, and hear an adult's fluent, easy reading.[3]

Jim Trelease expands on the importance of reluctant readers hearing fluent reading.

> If students are not read to, if day after day the only reading they hear is the drone of fellow members in the "turtle" reading group, they are certain to finish the year sounding like a "turtle." We need to balance the scales and let children know through reading aloud that there is more to reading than worksheets. . . . The child who is unaware of the riches of literature certainly can have no desire for them.[4]

I advocate reading the folktales in this book aloud instead of telling them from memory so that the students hear the phrasing of written rather than oral language. Written language is organized in complete sentences, while oral language is phrased in fragments, run-ons, and other less-formal structures that are perfectly correct in informal spoken English. Folktales provide a high-interest, fast-paced vehicle for exposing children to formal written English that is heard rather than seen. This is literature written in sentences and paragraphs of a quality far higher than that of the controlled-vocabulary books that young beginning readers (or older poor readers) can read independently.

By hearing and seeing these classic tales presented on the flannelboard the children reap benefits in the areas of vocabulary, motivation, and comprehension skills necessary for successful readers. They also gain in their writing skills. Teacher Mary Leonhardt explains:

> Poor readers write oral language rather than written language. Oral language and written language are very different. We use much looser grammatical structures when we talk—more compound sentences, plenty of fragments, few complex sentences. Plus, of course, we don't have to punctuate or spell when we talk. Students whose main language input is oral language will write these same loose, slightly awkward structures. They haven't been exposed to enough written language—saturated with enough written language—to acquire sophisticated written-language structures. And, of course, they don't punctuate or spell very adeptly.[5]

Poor readers need to be saturated with formal written language. Unfortunately, that is not the type of language they encounter in the short sentences of one- and two-syllable words used in their controlled-vocabulary reading textbooks. Just giving children high-quality text to read is not beneficial if their reading skills are on the level of decoding, slowly sounding out each word. One way to provide what these nonfluent readers need is for the teacher to expose them to written language by reading it aloud to them.

Fairy tales provide examples of prose that meet the conventional standards of formal written English while retaining some of the conversational devices and usages that will sound familiar to even the most nonliterate child. Although the stories in this book are written in a standard prose form and use formal English, the writing is "fairy tale English," which uses different vocabulary, phrases, and rhythm from other written prose. Like all formal written English, fairy tales have complete sentences that are organized into paragraphs and are arranged to progress logically. Unlike other formal written English, the prose in fairy tales retains the rhythm, the repetitions of parallel phrases, and the flow of speech. The writing should sound familiar and at the same time literate to the listener who has lived with storybooks as well as to the listener who has only lived with conversational language, the listener for whom literature is an unknown and unfamiliar novelty. What better vehicle for saturating a young child with formal traditional written English than the fairy tale, with its rich vocabulary, fast-paced plot, and spare prose phrased for oral presentation?

Selecting and Adapting the Tales

The tales chosen for this book come from diverse cultures around the world. Selected stories do not denigrate any group, such as stepmothers or little people. I researched multiple versions of the stories, using older published accounts rather than modern picture-book versions. From each variant I pulled out the most suitable or dramatic elements to make a version that when presented on the flannelboard would appeal to modern children. All the tales have plots and characters suitable for preschool or school-age children. In fact, they have enough complexity to hold the interest of children older than those who are usually considered ideal for flannelboard story telling; I have presented these tales in school and public library storytime programs for children ranging from ages three to eleven.

Let me explain my technique for writing prose to be read aloud. I composed these stories at the flannelboard, moving the felt figures and speaking aloud. I wrote what I said, and then I read it aloud again to revise and polish the sentences so they would sound more natural to the listener. I believe that a good flannelboard story cannot be written by a person sitting at a word processor or a typewriter. Stories written there sound like plain written prose. The stories need to be spoken first and then transcribed from the oral prose so they flow smoothly when read aloud. And that is the purpose of these stories—to be heard as read-alouds.

After I had written and revised, I field-tested the stories with groups of children in school and public library storytime programs. Then I revised the texts again on the basis of the children's response to them. Not all of the stories that I originally had chosen made it into this final version of the book. The ancient tales included here proved their suitability for modern children.

Value of the Flannelboard
for Presenting Tales

With so many educational benefits gained from reading stories aloud, why use the flannelboard to present them? Many teachers and researchers have written about the lack of imagination and visualization abilities in the nonfluent reader. This type of reader hears or reads the words but cannot conjure an image of the action taking place in the story. As a school librarian, I often asked students questions about stories that I had read to them or that they had read. Fluent readers, those who enjoyed reading, imagined a richly detailed, moving scene as they read or heard a story. While they were hearing or reading a story

they "entered" the story with their senses: seeing the actions, hearing characters talk, feeling characters' emotions, and perhaps even smelling elements of the setting. These fluent readers could describe the scenes and events of the story in detail. When I asked the poor readers what they saw when they heard or read a story, they would reply, "Nothing—there wasn't anything to see." These poor readers could enjoy stories presented on television or film, which supplied all the visual imagery for them. But when they heard or read a story, they did not see the action taking place.

The flannelboard gives these nonfluent readers a picture of some events in a story. Since the felt figures give only a partial representation of the characters and actions, the listeners' imaginations must supply the rest of the details and movement to complete the picture. In this way flannelboard stories serve as a bridge between totally provided visualization (watching television) and totally imagined visualization (listening or reading without illustrations).

The actions in these stories lend themselves to effective presentation with flannelboard figures. Many are cumulative tales, and one felt figure after another is added as the story unfolds. The stories were chosen specifically so that felt figures could be reused; that is, each character serves in several stories. Therefore, the storyteller needs to construct only a few felt figures to tell all eighteen stories.

Flannelboard Presentations

Making the Flannelboard
and Felt Figures

The Flannelboard

Although flannelboards can be bought, for several reasons I believe it is better to make them. First, most commercially available flannelboards are too small for storytelling. To present the stories in this book, it is necessary to use a board at least 30 inches wide and 56 inches long. A board larger than this size is even easier to use with these stories. Second, if you can find a commercial flannelboard this large, it will probably be prohibitively expensive. A homemade board can be constructed with materials that are free

or very inexpensive. Third, the commercially produced flannelboard will be much heavier than the homemade version, and it may not be the preferred color. A light blue or gray flannelboard visually enhances the colorful felt figures. Finally, the flannel on the homemade board may be removed easily for washing.

Make the flannelboard from a solid side of a large corrugated cardboard box or use a foam-core board that can be bought at an art- or office-supply store. Stretch two yards of a solid color cotton flannel over the board. Attach the flannel securely to the back of the board with masking tape.

Keep the flannelboard surface smooth. Felt figures do not adhere properly to a creased or folded flannelboard. Because your homemade flannelboard is lightweight and thin, it can be secured on top of a table with masking tape for storytelling and can be easily stored flat for later use.

The Felt Figures

The storytelling figures are made of glued-together pieces of colored felt. A few felt pieces require gold or silver glitter, gold thread, white kite string, or a small piece of aluminum foil. Refer to the step-by-step instructions and the patterns and color legends at the beginning of the Patterns section to cut and glue the figures. To cut the felt, use sharp fabric scissors that comfortably fit your hand.

Most patterns are shown full-sized. However, a few of the larger pieces are drawn at half scale and must be drawn to the given dimensions or enlarged 200 percent on a photocopier.

You may use either tracing paper or a photocopier to copy the full-scale patterns. If you use trac-ing paper, loosely cut around the traced pattern before pinning it to the felt. Then cut the traced pattern and felt simultaneously to ensure a crisp edge. If you use a photocopied pattern, cut it precisely on the pattern edge before pinning it to the felt and cutting.

Many patterns are symmetrical, and this is noted on the patterns by a dashed line. Select a piece of felt that is twice as large as the given pattern and fold it in half. Place the dashed line of the pattern on the felt fold and pin the pattern in place. Then cut through the two layers of felt along the solid line of the pattern.

Assemble the felt pieces according to the illustration for each completed felt figure. (Completed figures are numbered in the pattern section.) It is important to preassemble all of the felt pieces for one figure, noting where the pieces overlap, before beginning to glue them together. Start with the larger pieces and use a thick, white tacky glue that is recommended specifically for felt. For best results, test the glue on a scrap of felt first. (The glue must be thick enough to not soak into the felt.)

When the glued figures are dry, draw eyes and details as shown on the patterns with a black felt-tip marker. Use a series of dots to draw a line on the felt figures. (A solid line will raise the nap on the felt causing undesirable results.)

When each figure is completed and dry, put a small label on the back and number it according to the List of Felt Figures. (Only very small labels will not prevent a figure from properly adhering to the flannelboard.) A numbered small piece of masking tape will also work fine.

The two reversible figures are the Cottage and the Rich House. Their numbers can be easily remembered or the numbered labels can be removed temporarily for storytelling.

Many of the felt figures are used in more than one story. Store the figures in numerical order and they can be quickly accessible for the next storytelling. After each storytelling session a review of the numbers will confirm that all figures are accounted for. Protect the felt figures by storing them in a large, moisture-proof container. Small figures with glitter can be protected in sealed plastic bags. When stored carefully, these felt figures will last through many years of storytelling.

Setting Up

Before the presentation, set the flannelboard on a table against a wall with light shining on the board. Let the board tilt backward at a slight angle to the table. (If the board is perfectly vertical, the felt figures will fall off during the story, which is extremely distracting for the audience.) Fasten the bottom of the board to the table with masking tape to keep it from sliding.

Arrange the felt figures on the table from left to right and top to bottom in the order in which they will be used to illustrate the story. (The Set-Up Instructions for each tale list the figures in sequence.) Each time you need to add a figure to the board, pick up the last piece on the left. If the figures are in order, you can continue reading the text without looking away from it; just take the figure on the end, knowing it will be correct. A description at the beginning of each story tells you which felt figures should be on the board before you begin to read.

Rehearsing

Rehearse the story before you present it to an audience. When telling a story, you will need to stand to one side of the flannelboard and face the audience. (If you are seated, you will probably have to stand up or at least stretch uncomfortably to reach the felt figures on the far end of the table every time a piece is added or moved.) While standing, you can reach any felt figure on the table or flannelboard with minimal movement, thereby minimizing audience distraction from the story.

Hold the story text in one hand and move the felt figures with the other hand. When you need to use two hands to move a large felt figure, set the text on a corner of the table while you move the figures. When you remove a felt figure from the board, set it on the end of the table where it will be available if it is needed again.

Practice moving the felt figures while reading the story aloud. Narrate the story in your natural reading voice; do not use a regional or ethnic dialect for the characters in the story. Imitation dialect comes across as patronizing or belittling to the group that speaks that form of the language.

To differentiate between the voices of different characters in the story, consistently use a higher or a lower pitch or a faster or a slower delivery for individual characters. To help you maintain each character's voice, the name of the speaking character has been written before the line of dialogue. For example, the stories use "Grandfather said, 'We need a little help,'" rather than "'We need a little help,' said Grandfather." This prepares you for a change of voice and tells the listener, who of course cannot see the quotation marks written around the dialogue, that a character is speaking the words.

Using the Text

Story Introductions

The introductions that precede each story include information about the source of the tale, although nobody knows the true origin of any folktale. Most were collected and published in written form by folklorists and authors in the eighteenth, nineteenth, and twentieth centuries after being passed down for hundreds of years through the oral tradition.

At the beginning of the eighteenth century, Charles Perrault published collections of European tales that were soon translated from French into English. The French governess Marie Leprince de Beaumont wrote her distinctive retellings of European folktales in the early eighteenth century. By the early nineteenth century the brothers Wilhelm and Jacob Grimm published their collections of stories that had been recounted orally in Germany. The Grimms' retellings have been translated widely; they are among the best-known traditional tales now in English-speaking countries.

During the twentieth century Harold Courlander published several collections of West African tales. By the late twentieth century folklorists began collecting stories that are still being told by Native Americans throughout the Americas. Many less famous folklorists and authors have researched and published folktales from diverse places throughout the world.

The Introduction to each story names some of the places where the tale has been recorded, which does not imply that the tale originated there. The origins of all these folktales are lost in the preliterate times in which they were first told.

The Script and Pacing

The eighteen stories for flannelboard presentation are printed in a two-column format. The text to be read aloud is on the left and the directions for figure placements on the flannelboard are on the right (beside the words being read at the time of each placement). This arrangement enables you to present the stories successfully with a minimum of preparation and rehearsal.

The stories are paced so that the text and matching movements are balanced. There are no long reading passages without corresponding movement of the figures, and there are no movements without accompanying text. These techniques and the text format were adapted and improved during my years as a teacher and a school librarian.

Follow-up Activities

After presenting the story, you may want to introduce the children to other retellings of the same story in picture books, film, and other media. Invite children to discuss their experiences with different versions by comparing and contrasting the settings, characters, and plots. Depending on the maturity of the group, you may want to locate on a world map some of the places where the story has been told.

Each folktale in this book is followed by suggestions for extending the themes developed in the story. The Questions for Discussion and Writing help promote higher level thinking. They require answers beyond "yes" or "no" or a mere recounting of what happened in the story. Instead, they require some thought, and they invite differences of opinion.

A game or other activity follows the questions. Some of the activities reinforce school instructional goals, such as sequencing events and following directions. The required materials are items commonly found in classrooms or public libraries. Projects can be completed in fifteen or twenty minutes, with little adult supervision, and allow completion during a half-hour public library storytime.

Other activities are games that emphasize cooperation rather than competition. They encourage constant participation of all group members rather than long periods of time waiting for a turn. Although adults may not understand the point of playing a game in which nobody wins or loses, children enter into these games with the same motivation that carries them through hours of "playing house" and other repetitive activities of "let's pretend." The students in my library storytimes participated with enthusiasm in the games presented in this book, and only those activities that were proven successful with large groups of children in my school and public library programs have been included.

The Recommended Read-Aloud Books sections include both old favorites from the library and new publications that are currently in print. The stories and illustrations feature cultures throughout the world as well as the diverse people of our own country. Both stories with illustrations and those with few or none are included, ranging from some picture books suitable mainly for preschoolers to some longer stories for older elementary school students. All the picture books listed have pictures large enough for a group to see from a distance in a classroom or library. Each has enough text to make an effective read-aloud presentation. All the recommended books have been proven to hold a group's attention.

The flannelboard stories and their accompanying introductory and follow-up materials should provide busy teachers and librarians with several complete storytime sessions, along with games for recess or for playing later at home. They require minimal advance-preparation time and very little money for materials or equipment.

Notes

1. W. H. Auden, review of *Grimms' Fairy Tales, The New York Times,* 12 Nov. 1944, quoted in Zena Sutherland and May Hill Arbuthnot, *Chil-dren and Books* (Glenview, Ill.: Scott, Foresman, 1986), 177.

2. Jim Trelease, *The New Read-Aloud Handbook* (New York: Penguin, 1989), 2.

3. May Hill Arbuthnot, *Time for Fairy Tales, Old and New* (Chicago: Scott, Foresman, 1961), x–xi.

4. Trelease, *Handbook,* 12.

5. Mary Leonhardt, *Parents Who Love Reading, Kids Who Don't: How It Happens and What You Can Do about It* (New York: Crown, 1993), 14–15.

I

Patterns

List of Felt Figures

continued

Objects *continued*

Supply List

1. Tracing paper and pencil
2. Ultrafine- or fine-point black felt-tip marker
3. Sharp fabric scissors
4. Straight pins
5. Thick, white tacky glue labeled for use on felt
6. Gold thread
7. Gold and silver glitter
8. Small piece of aluminum foil
9. Nine-inch piece of white kite string
10. Many colors of felt (see color legend)

Patterns Legend

cut line _____
Cut the patterns on the solid line.

fold line - - - - - - - - - - - -
Place the dashed line on the fold of the felt before cutting. The pattern is symmetrical.

Cut 2—Make two pieces from the same pattern (or 5, if "cut 5")

Color Legend

W	White
C	Cream
T	Tan
Y	Yellow
G	Gold
GBr	Golden Brown
Br	Brown
O	Orange
YGn	Yellow Green
Gn	Green
DGn	Dark Green
LB	Light Blue
B	Blue
RB	Royal Blue
BGy	Blue Gray
Gy	Gray
P	Pink
RP	Rose Pink
M	Magenta
V	Violet
Pr	Purple
R	Red
Bk	Black

Enlarging

Most patterns are drawn at full scale. A few patterns that are too large to fit on a page are reduced to half scale. These are labeled to enlarge and must be drawn twice as large using the actual dimensions provided or photocopied at 200 percent.

Photocopying

1. Large patterns drawn at half scale can be enlarged 200 percent on a photocopier. Use 11-inch by 17-inch copy paper and copy half the pieces on a page at a time.

2. If you prefer to photocopy the full-scale patterns, cut the copied patterns precisely on the cutting line before pinning them to the felt. Do not cut copy paper and felt simultaneously.

3. Three felt figures have Old English lettering on the patterns. Photocopy, cut out the words, then glue them to the finished felt figure. (If you prefer, the words can be handwritten on paper.)

Step-by-Step Instructions

1. Choose only one felt figure and study its illustration.

2. Trace the patterns that make up the pieces of the figure following any specific instructions.

3. Cut loosely around the traced pattern.

4. Pin the traced pattern to the desired color of felt noting if there is a fold line.

5. Cut through the tracing paper and the felt simultaneously to ensure a crisp edge.

6. After all the colored felt pieces are cut out, lay out and assemble them according to the figure illustration, noting where the pieces overlap.

7. After everything looks correct, glue larger pieces first and the smallest details last. Be sure to test glue on a piece of scrap felt. It should be thick enough to not soak into felt, so it will bond quickly. Some glues have directions for thickening the glue.

8. After the felt figure is dry, draw details with a black felt-tip marker. Use only dots. A series of dots will draw a line.

9. Let the figure dry overnight.

10. Number the completed figure on the back with a small label to correspond with the list of felt figures.

Easy Tips

1. Use pinking shears to cut scallop-edged patterns quickly.

2. Cut small-detail patterns, such as mouths, noses, rocks, and rosebuds, freehand.

3. For easy cleanup, apply glue to felt pieces with a flat wooden ice cream bar stick. A toothpick works well for small detail pieces.

1. Castle

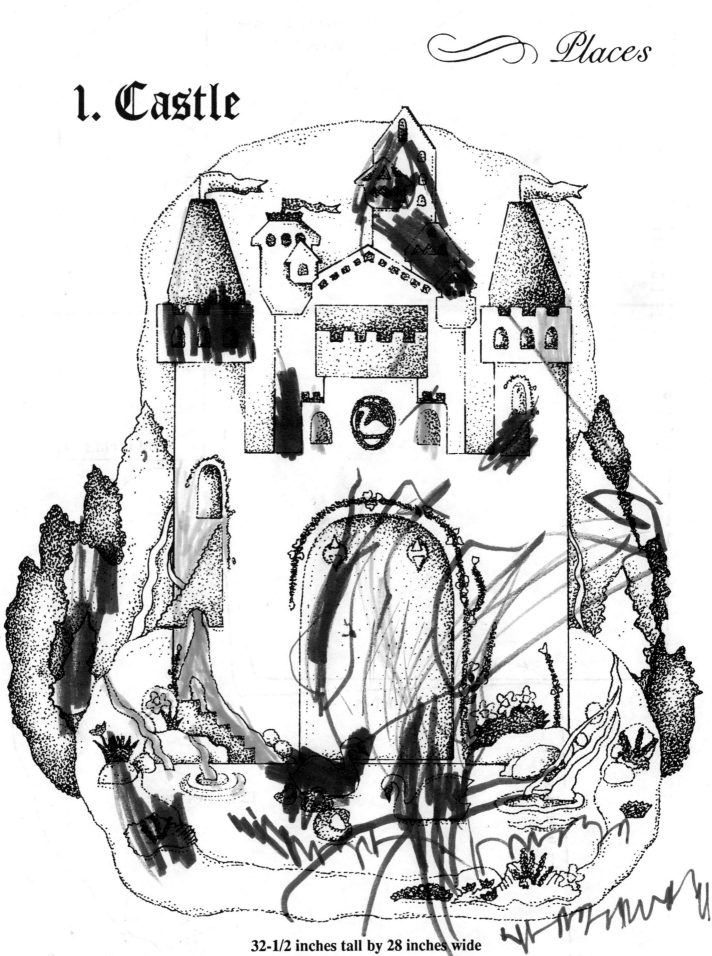

32-1/2 inches tall by 28 inches wide
Add more climbing roses, rocks,
and flowers if you wish.

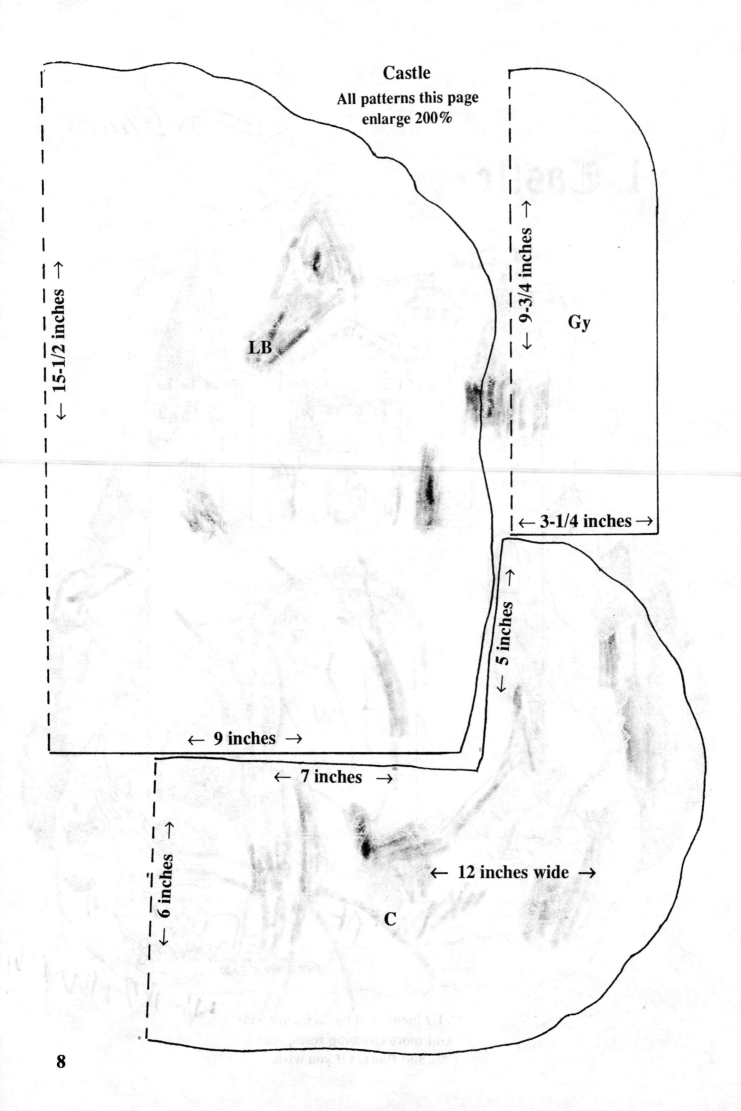

Castle

**All patterns this page
enlarge 200%**

← 15-1/2 inches →

LB

← 9-3/4 inches →

Gy

← 3-1/4 inches →

← 5 inches →

← 9 inches →

← 7 inches →

← 6 inches →

← 12 inches wide →

C

8

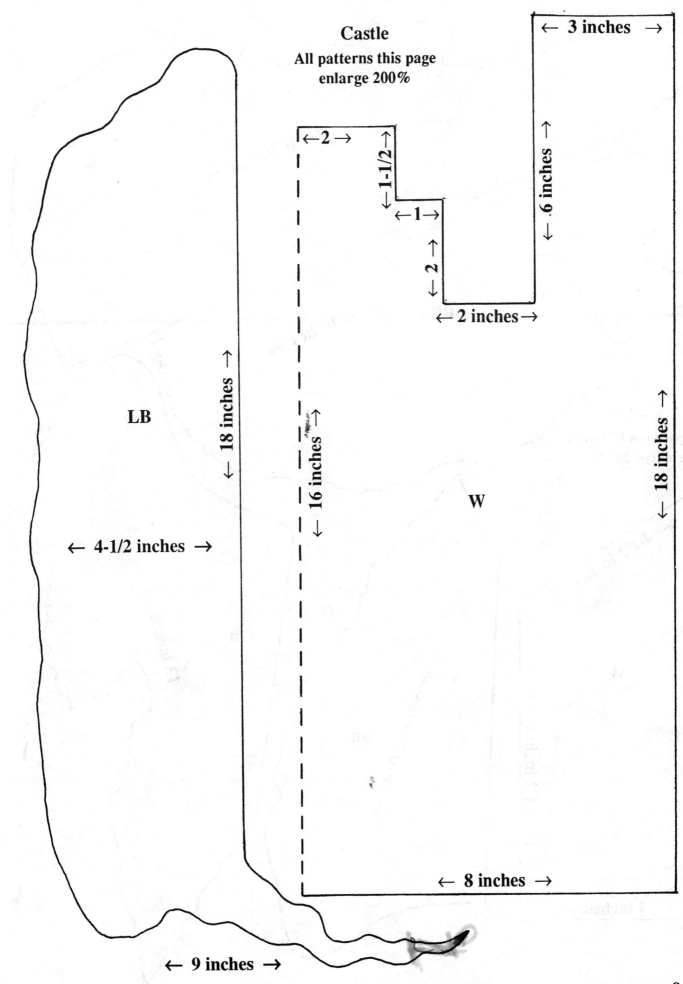

Castle

All patterns this page
enlarge 200%

← 3 inches →

← 2 →

← 1-1/2 →

← 1 →

← 2 →

← .6 inches →

← 2 inches →

↑ 18 inches ↓

LB

← 4-1/2 inches →

↑ 16 inches ↓

W

↑ 18 inches ↓

← 8 inches →

← 9 inches →

9

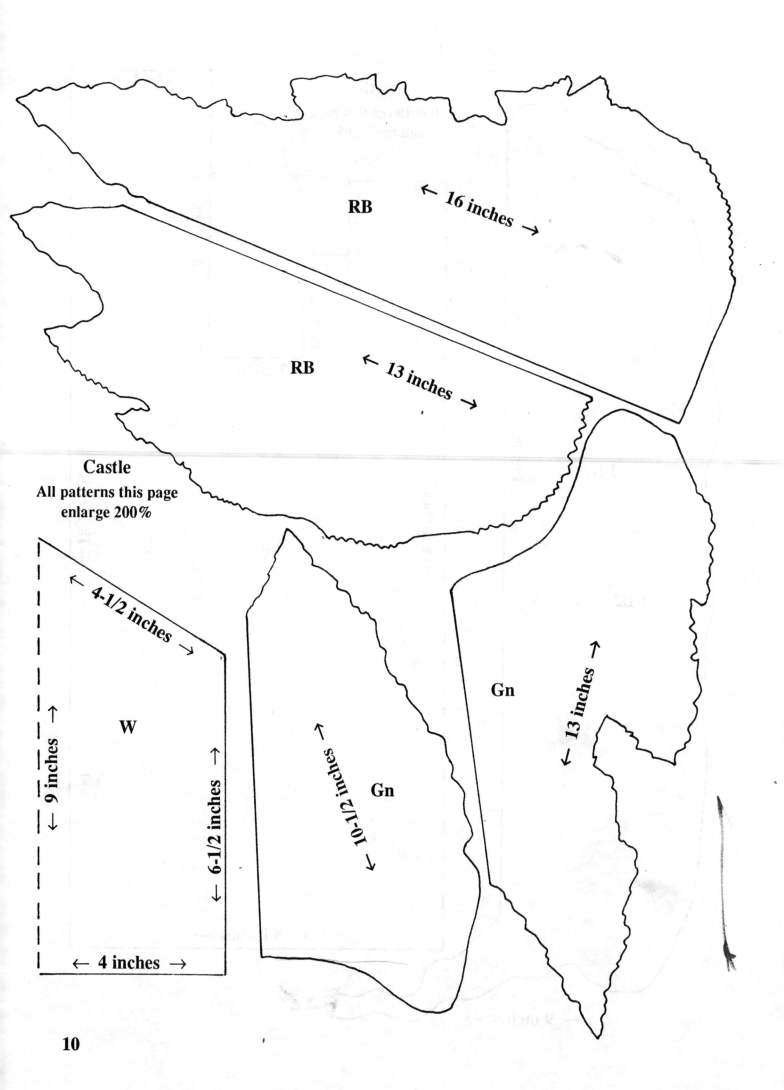

RB

← 16 inches →

RB

← 13 inches →

Castle

All patterns this page
enlarge 200%

← 4-1/2 inches →

↑ 9 inches ↓

W

↑ 6-1/2 inches ↓

↑ 10-1/2 inches ↓

Gn

Gn

↑ 13 inches ↓

← 4 inches →

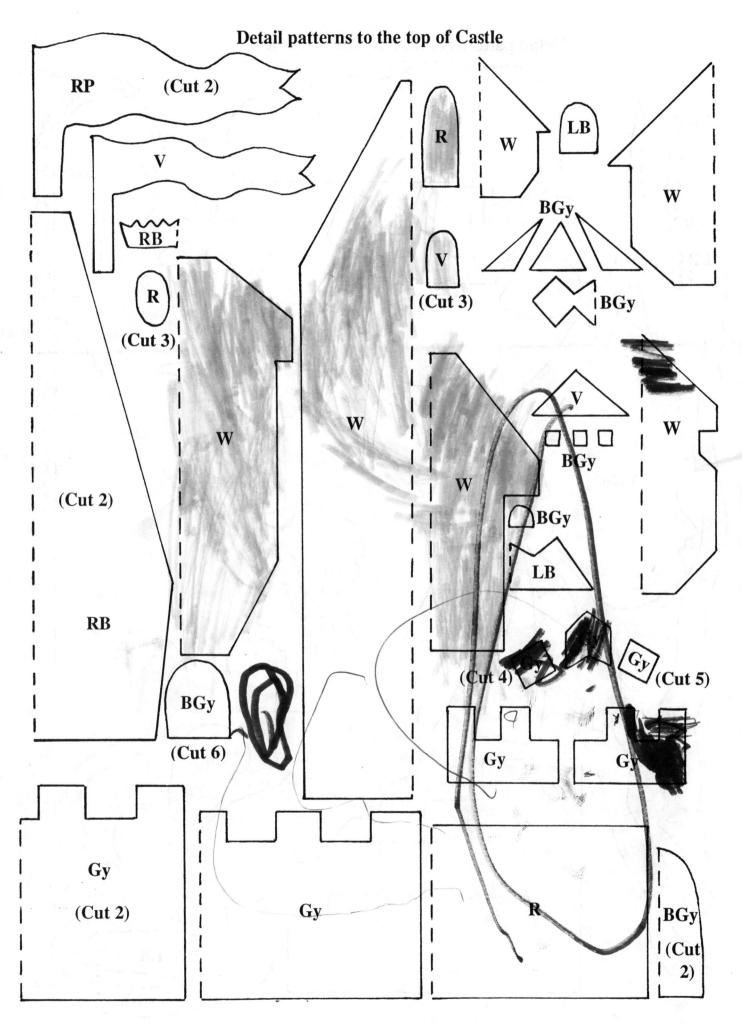

Detail patterns to the top of Castle

RP (Cut 2)

V

RB

R (Cut 3)

(Cut 2)

RB

W

R (Cut 3)

V (Cut 3)

BGy

W LB

W

BGy BGy

V

BGy

W

W

W

BGy

LB

(Cut 4) Gy (Cut 5)

Gy Gy

Gy

BGy (Cut 6)

Gy (Cut 2)

Gy

R

BGy (Cut 2)

Detail patterns to the left side of Castle

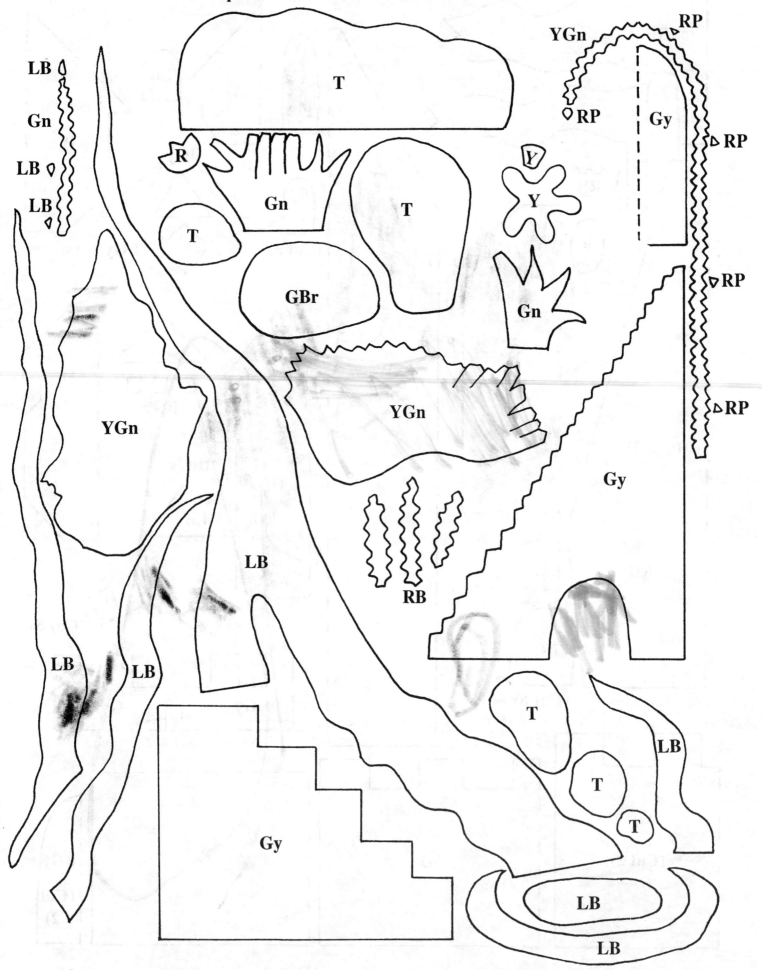

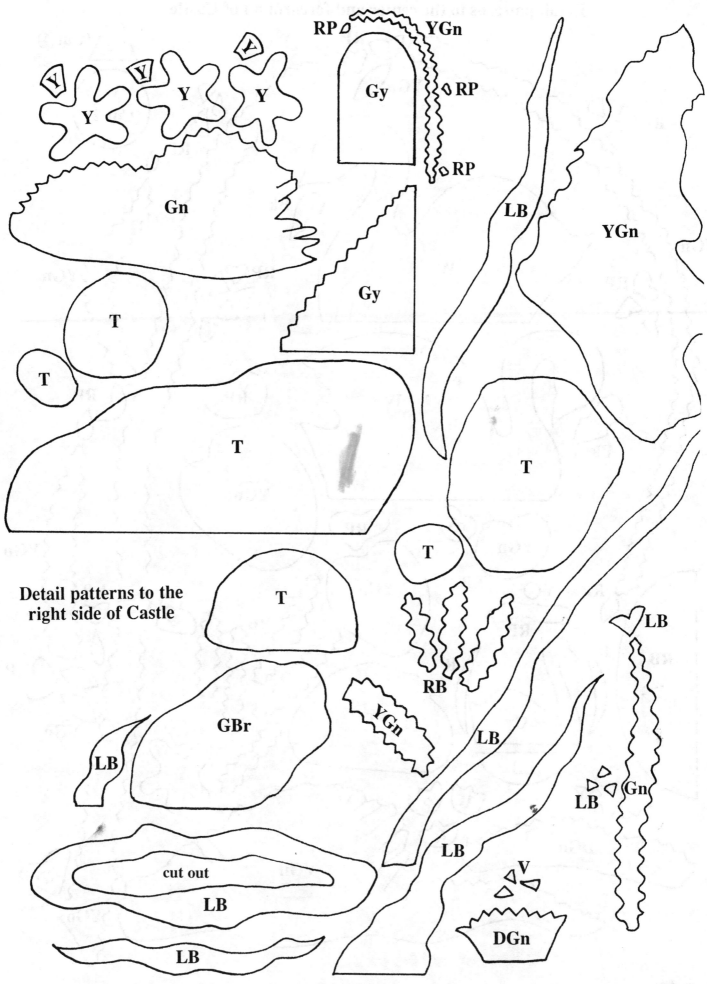

Y

Y

Y

Y

Y

Y

RP   YGn

Gy

RP

RP

Gn

LB

YGn

T

T

Gy

T

T

Detail patterns to the right side of Castle

T

T

RB

LB

YGn

GBr

LB

LB

LB

Gn

LB

cut out

LB

LB

V

LB

DGn

13

Detail patterns to the center and foreground of Castle

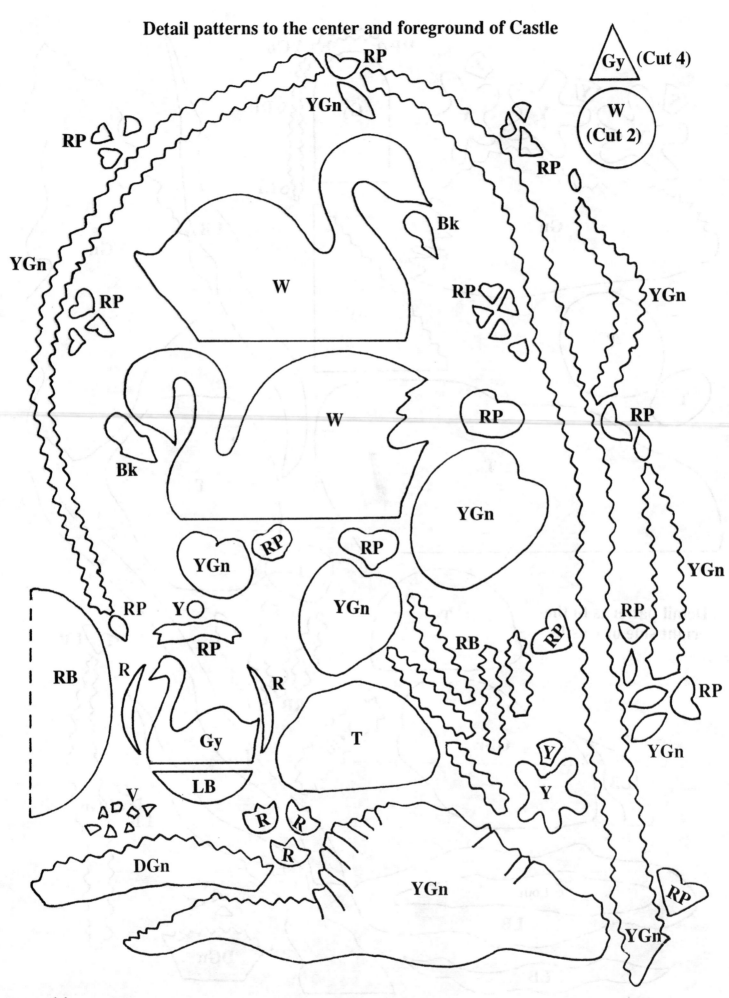

Gy (Cut 4)

W (Cut 2)

RP

YGn

RP

YGn

RP

Bk

RP

YGn

RP

YGn

RP

W

Bk

W

RP

YGn

YGn

RP

YGn

RP

YGn

YGn

RB

RP

Y

RB

RP

RP

R

R

Gy

T

RP

RB

RP

RP

Y

Y

RP

YGn

V

R R

LB

R

DGn

YGn

YGn

RP

YGn

2. Distant Castle

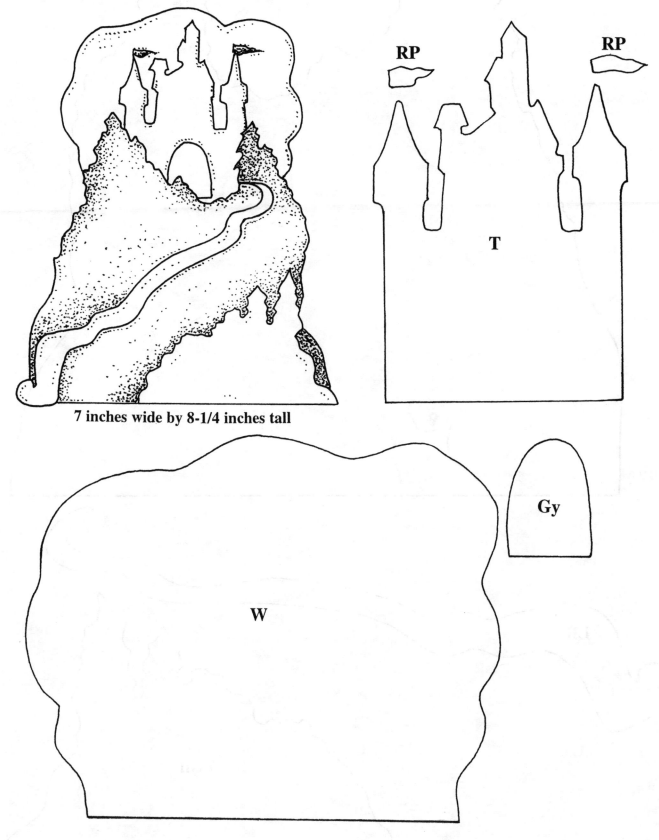

7 inches wide by 8-1/4 inches tall

RP

RP

T

Gy

W

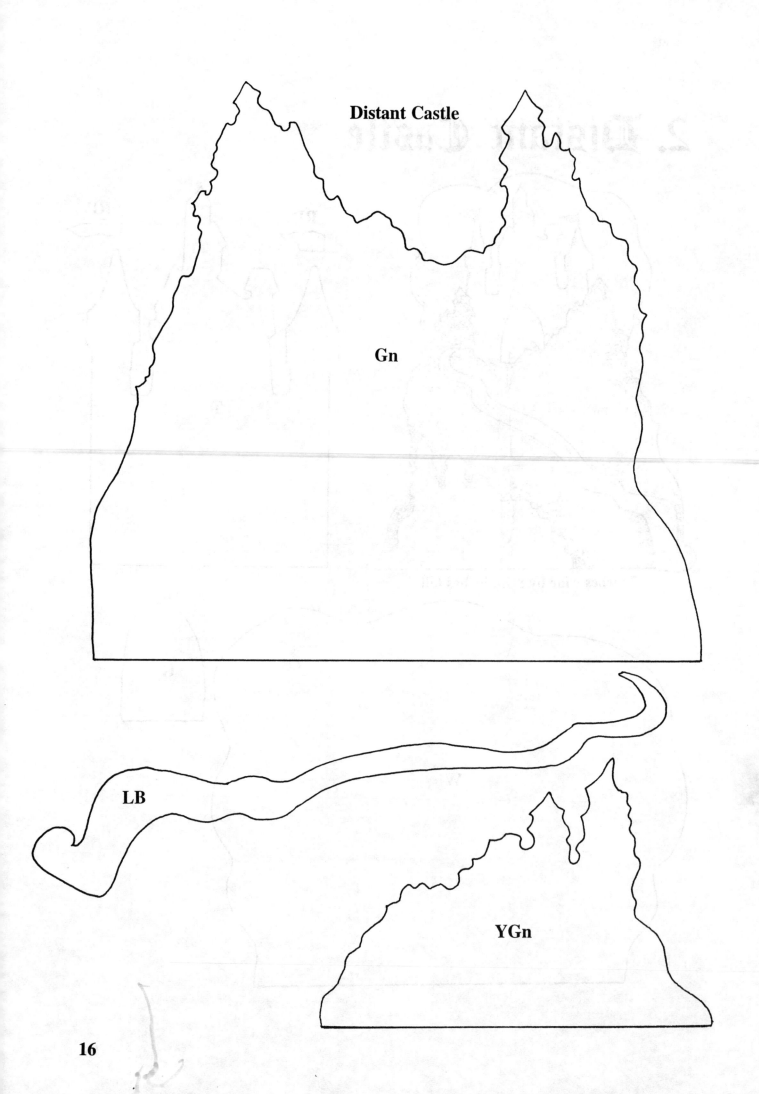

Distant Castle

Gn

LB

YGn

3. Tower

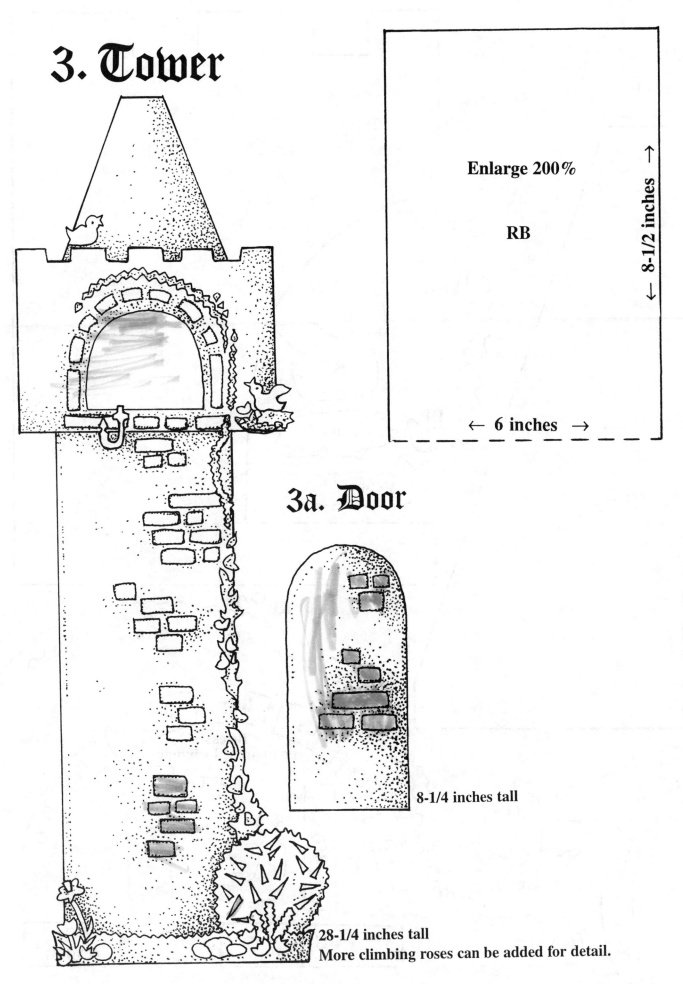

Enlarge 200%

RB

← 8-1/2 inches →

← 6 inches →

3a. Door

8-1/4 inches tall

28-1/4 inches tall
More climbing roses can be added for detail.

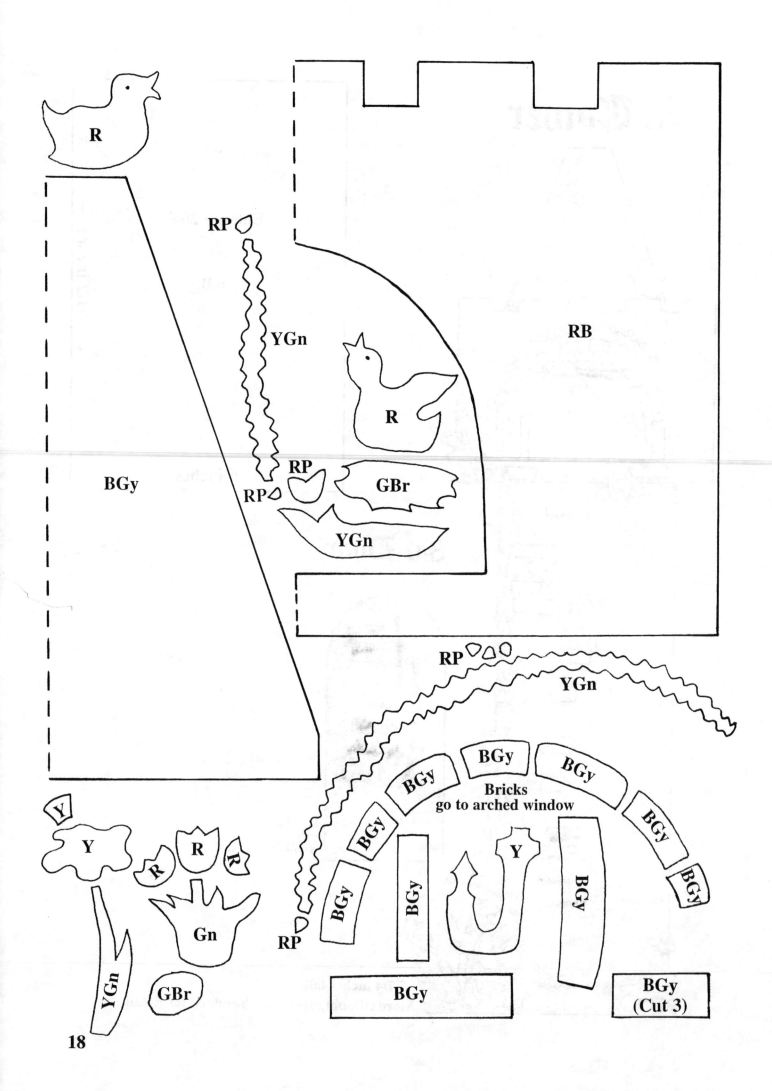

R

RP

YGn

RB

R

RP

GBr

YGn

BGy

RP

RP

YGn

RP

YGn

BGy

BGy

BGy

Bricks
go to arched window

BGy

BGy

BGy

BGy

BGy

Y

R

R

R

Gn

Y

Y

BGy

BGy

YGn

GBr

18

BGy

BGy
(Cut 3)

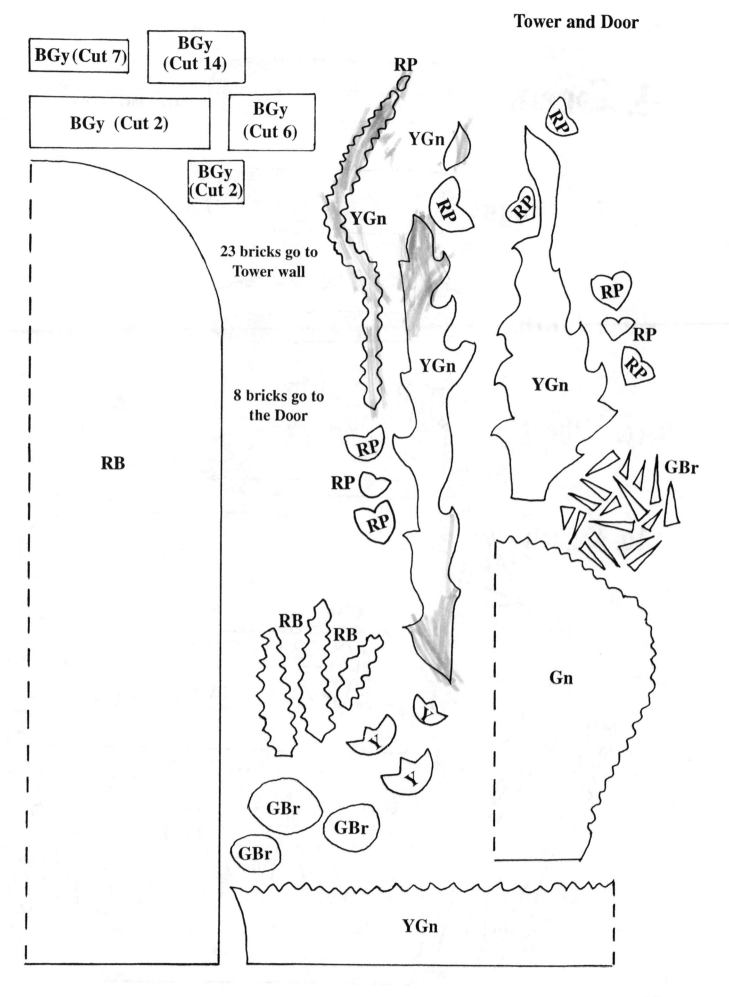

BGy (Cut 7)

BGy (Cut 14)

BGy (Cut 2)

BGy (Cut 6)

BGy (Cut 2)

RP

YGn

YGn

RP

RP

RP

RP

RP

RP

RP

23 bricks go to Tower wall

YGn

YGn

GBr

8 bricks go to the Door

RP

RP

RP

RB

RB

RB

Gn

Y

Y

Y

GBr

GBr

GBr

YGn

19

4. Seeds

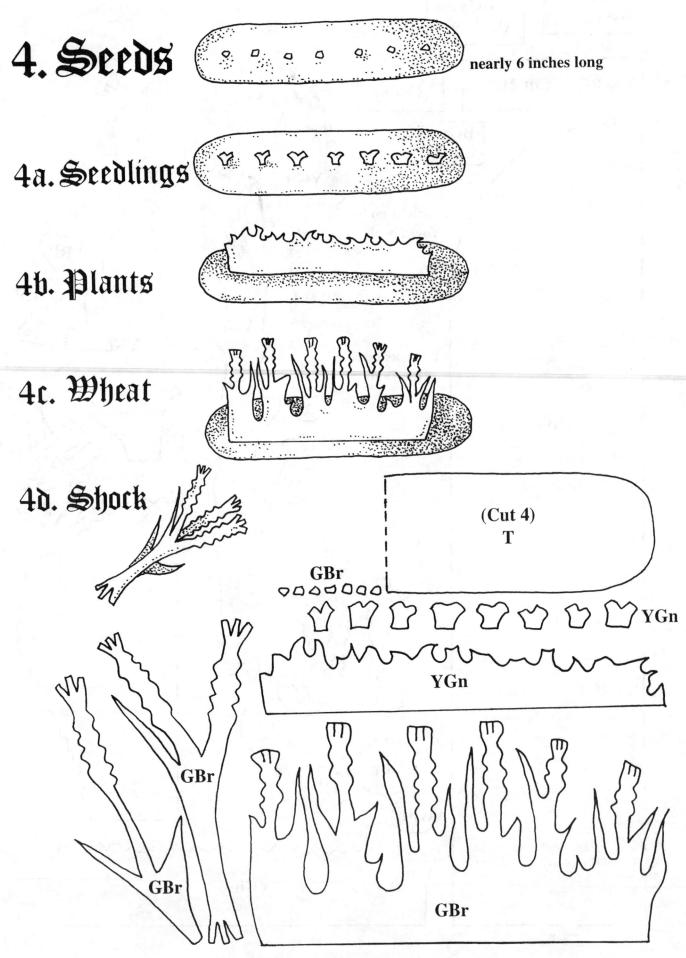

nearly 6 inches long

4a. Seedlings

4b. Plants

4c. Wheat

4d. Shock

GBr

(Cut 4)
T

YGn

YGn

GBr

GBr

GBr

5. Garden

9-1/4 inches long by 7-1/2 inches tall

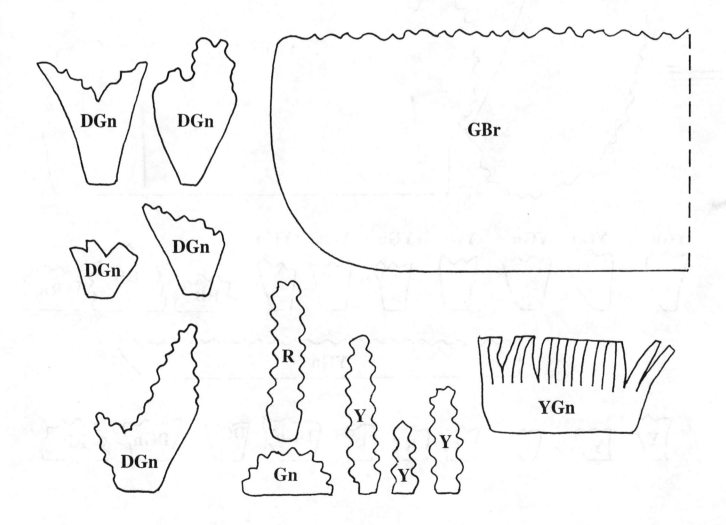

DGn

DGn

DGn

DGn

GBr

DGn

R

Gn

Y

Y

Y

YGn

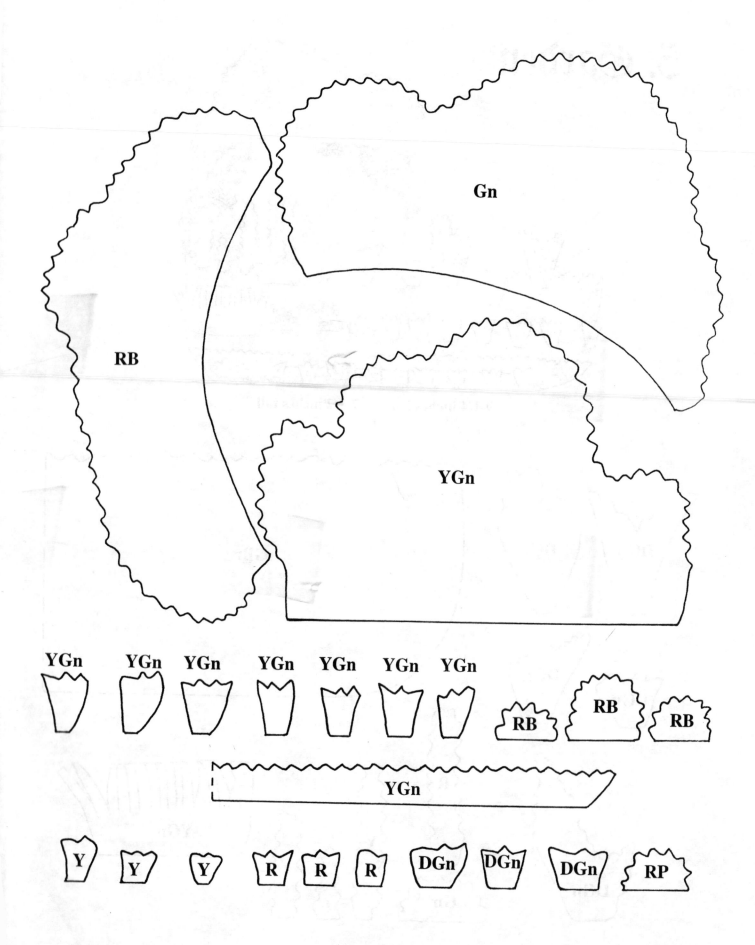

6. Forest

14 inches tall by 15-1/2 inches wide

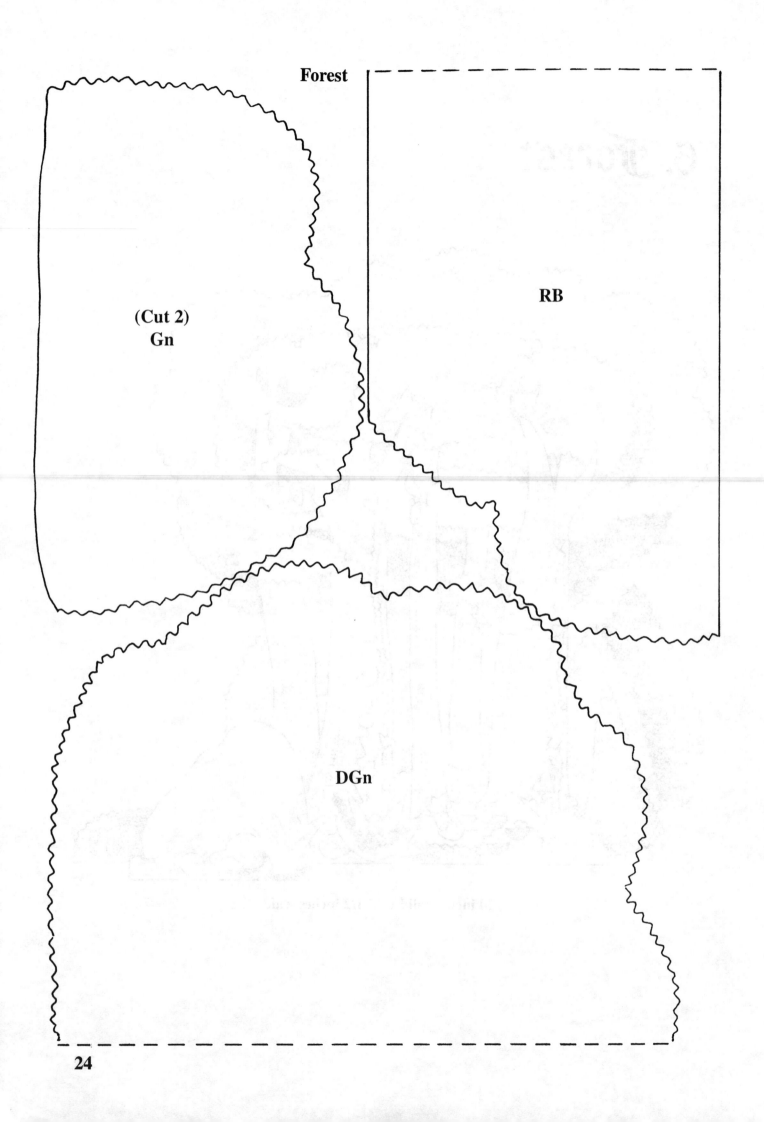

Forest

RB

(Cut 2)
Gn

DGn

24

Forest

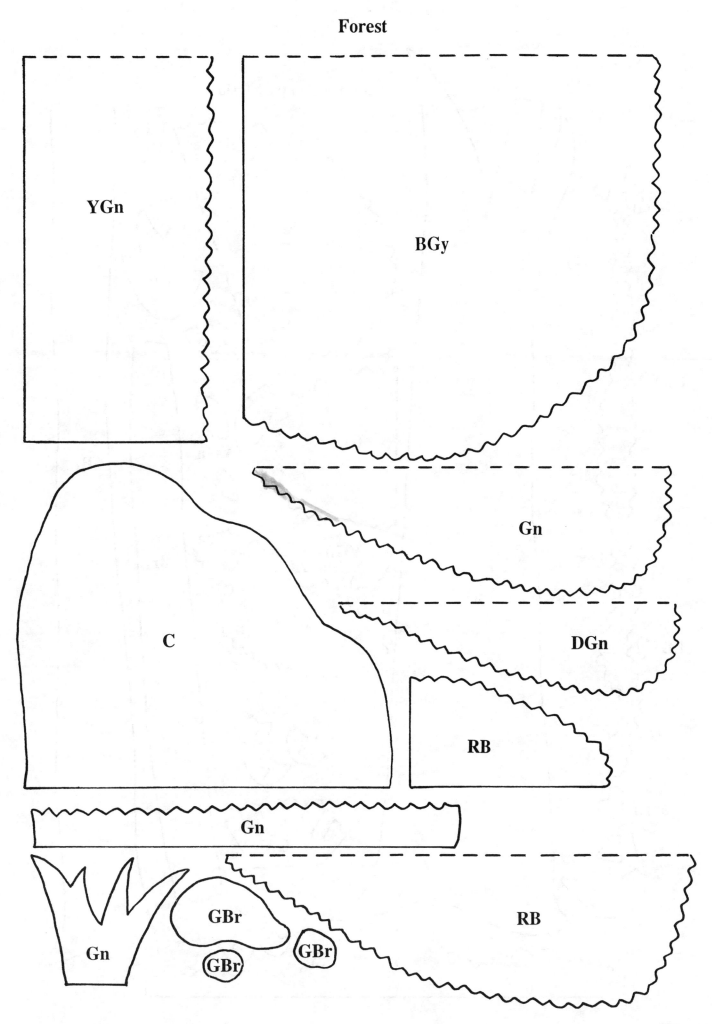

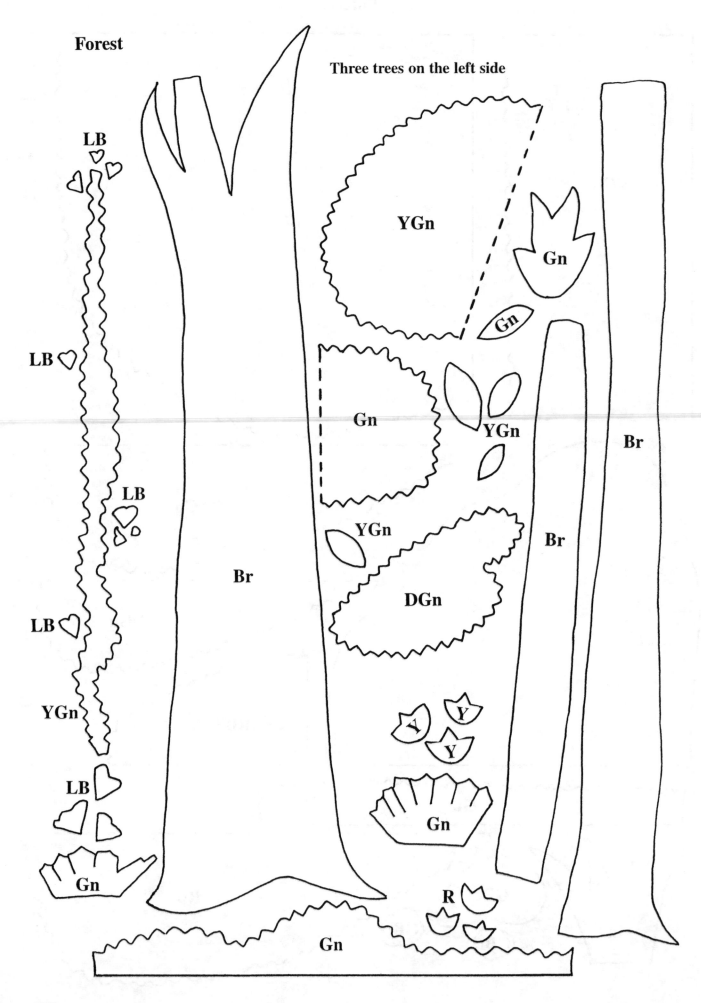

Forest

Three trees on the left side

LB

LB

LB

LB

YGn

LB

Gn

YGn

Gn

Br

YGn

Gn

Gn

YGn

DGn

Br

Br

Br

Y

Y

Y

Gn

R

Gn

26

Forest

Two trees on the right side

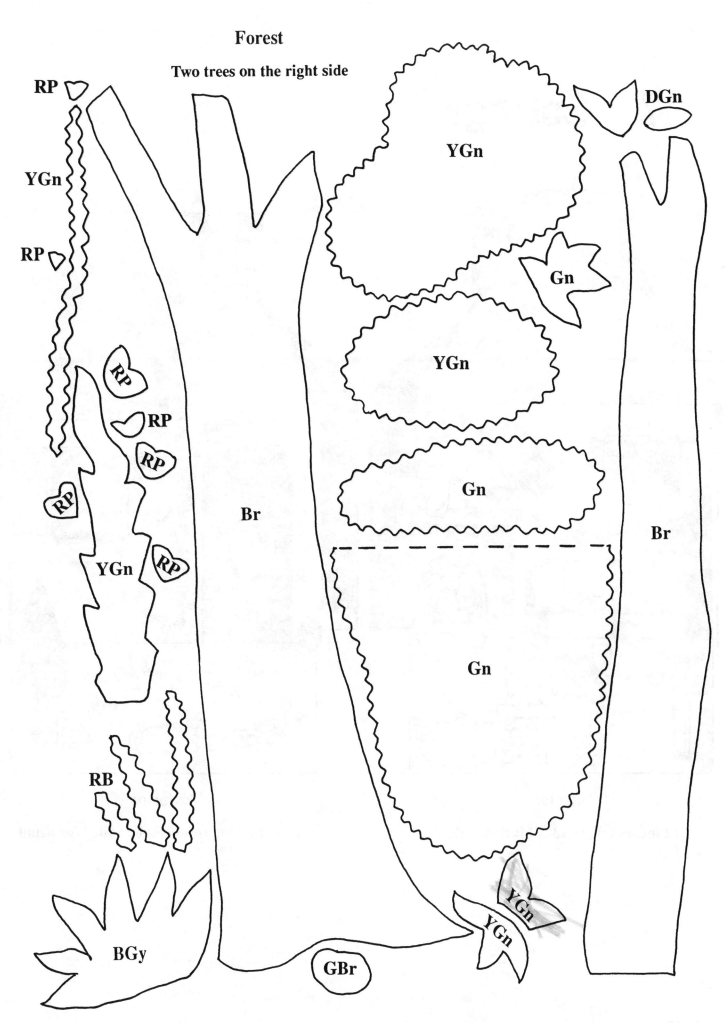

RP

YGn

RP

RP

RP

RP

RP

RP

YGn

RB

BGy

Br

GBr

YGn

YGn

DGn

YGn

Gn

YGn

Gn

Gn

Br

27

7. Cottage

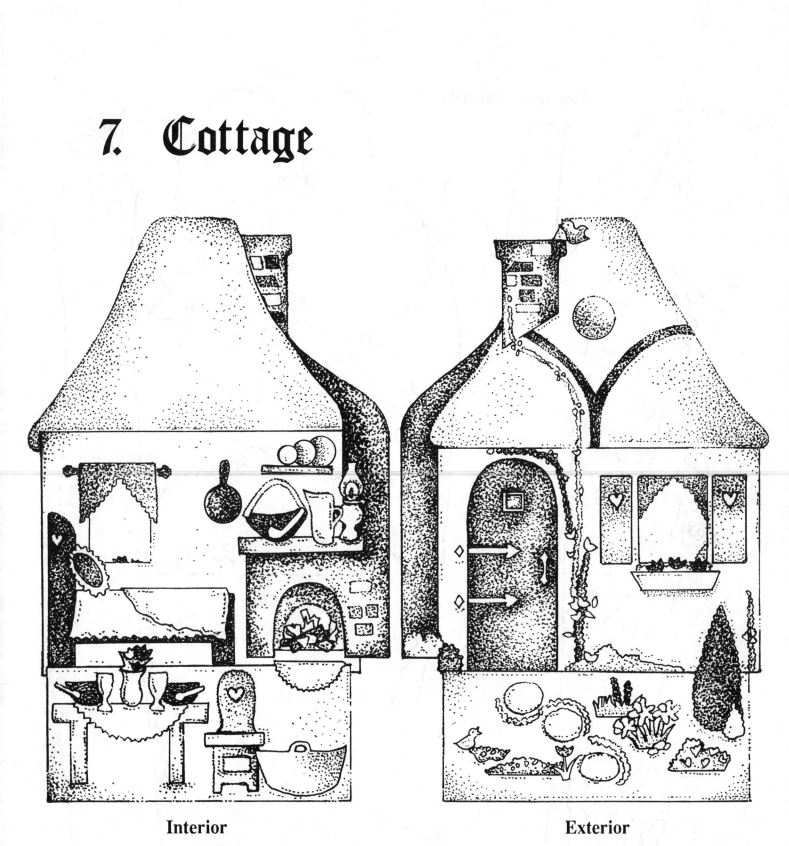

Interior

22 inches tall by 13-3/4 inches wide

Exterior

More climbing roses can be added for detail.

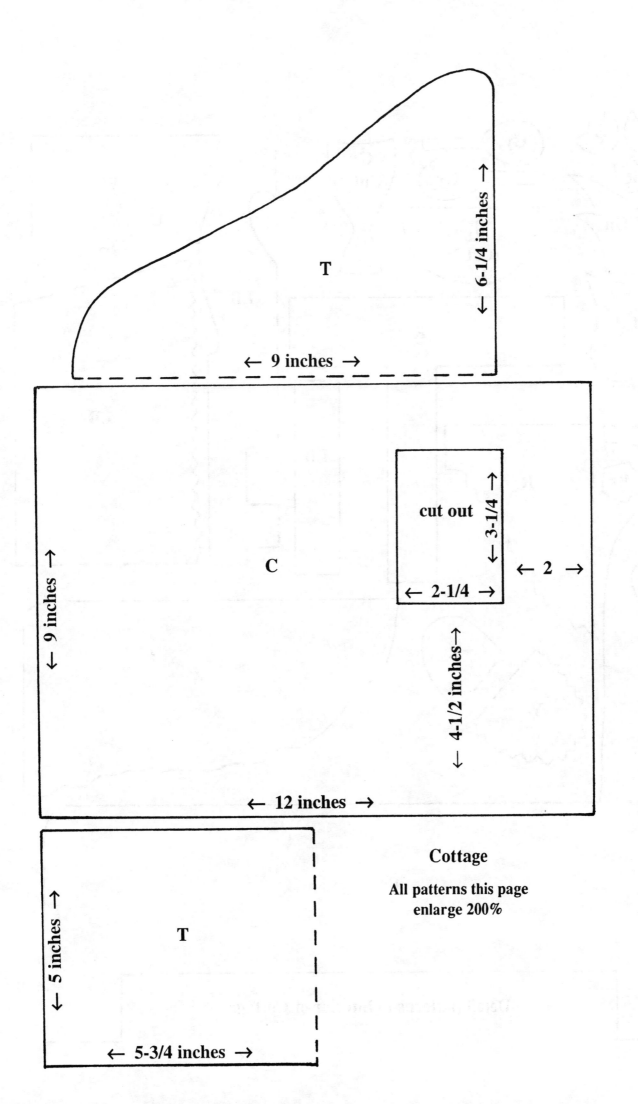

T

← 6-1/4 inches →

← 9 inches →

cut out

← 3-1/4 →

C

← 2-1/4 →

← 2 →

← 9 inches →

← 4-1/2 inches →

← 12 inches →

T

← 5 inches →

← 5-3/4 inches →

Cottage

**All patterns this page
enlarge 200%**

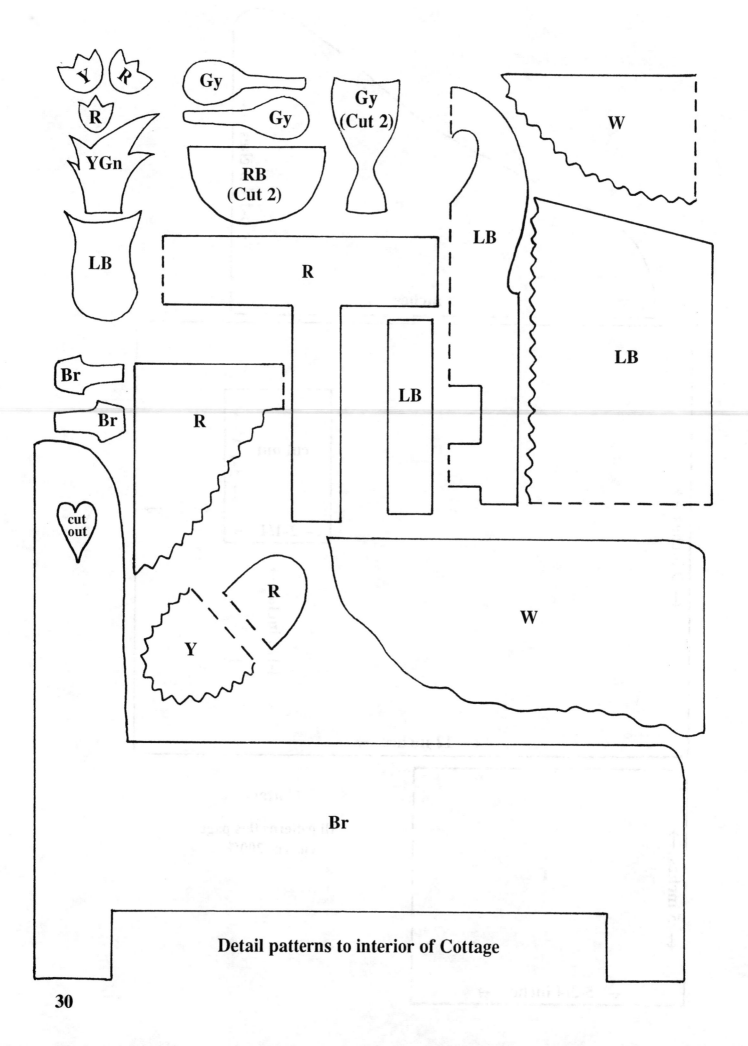

Detail patterns to interior of Cottage

30

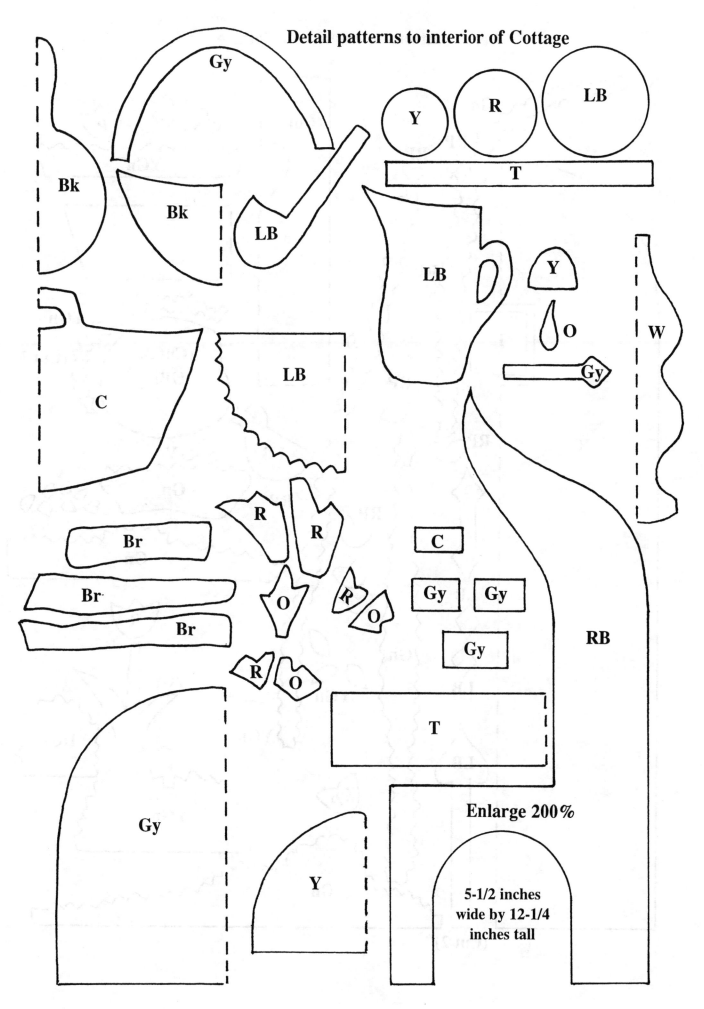

Detail patterns to interior of Cottage

Enlarge 200%

5-1/2 inches
wide by 12-1/4
inches tall

31

Detail patterns to exterior of Cottage

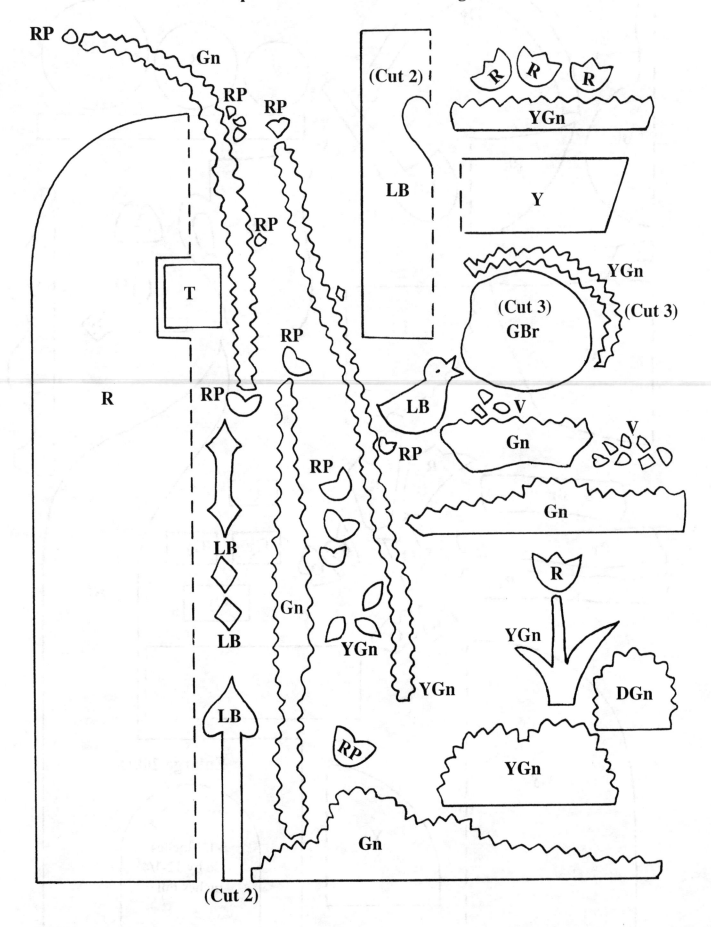

RP

Gn

RP

RP

RP

(Cut 2)

LB

R R R

YGn

Y

YGn

(Cut 3)
GBr

(Cut 3)

RP

T

RP

R

RP

RP

LB

LB

RP

LB

RP

Gn

YGn

YGn

RP

LB

V

Gn

V

Gn

R

YGn

DGn

YGn

RP

Gn

(Cut 2)

Detail patterns to exterior of Cottage

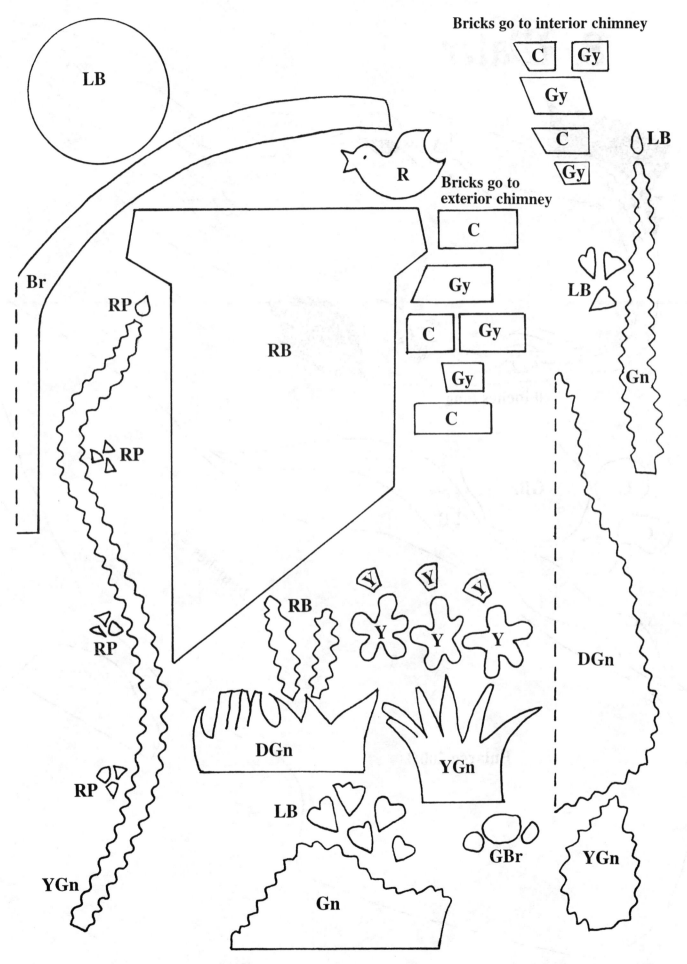

Bricks go to interior chimney

Bricks go to exterior chimney

LB

Br

RP

RB

RP

RP

RP

YGn

C   Gy

Gy

C

Gy

LB

C

Gy

C   Gy

Gy

C

LB

Gn

R

Y   Y   Y

RB

Y   Y   Y

DGn

DGn

YGn

DGn

LB

GBr

YGn

Gn

8. Water

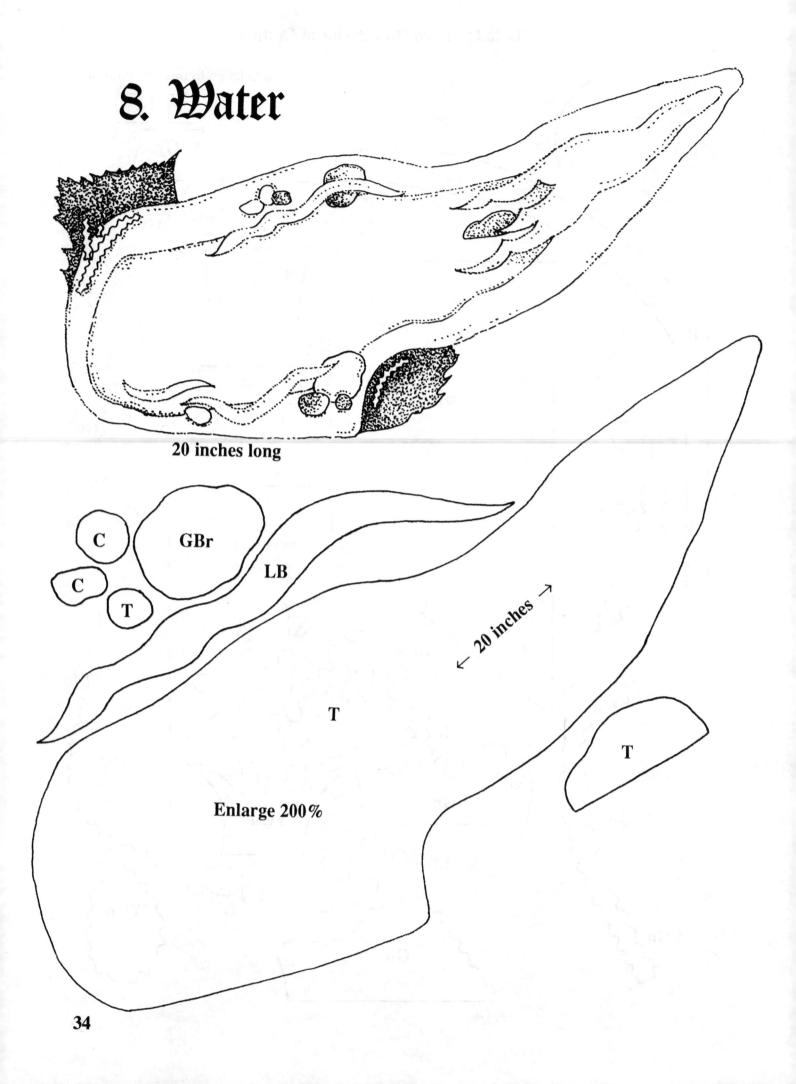

20 inches long

C

C

GBr

T

LB

← 20 inches →

T

Enlarge 200%

T

34

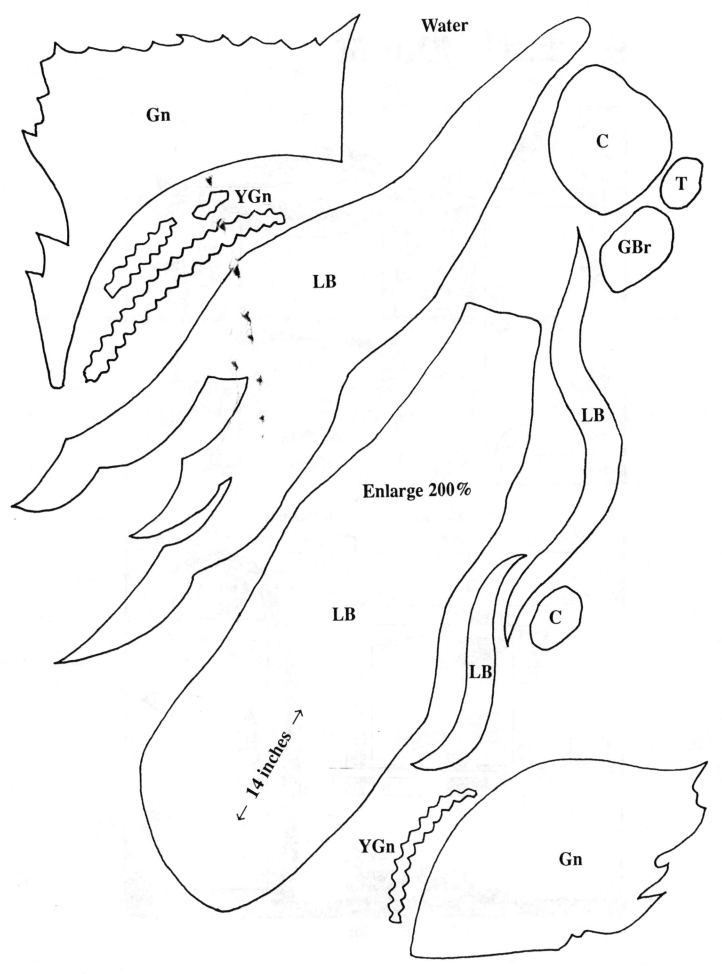

Water

Gn

YGn

C

T

GBr

LB

LB

Enlarge 200%

LB

C

LB

LB

← 14 inches →

YGn

Gn

9. Rich House

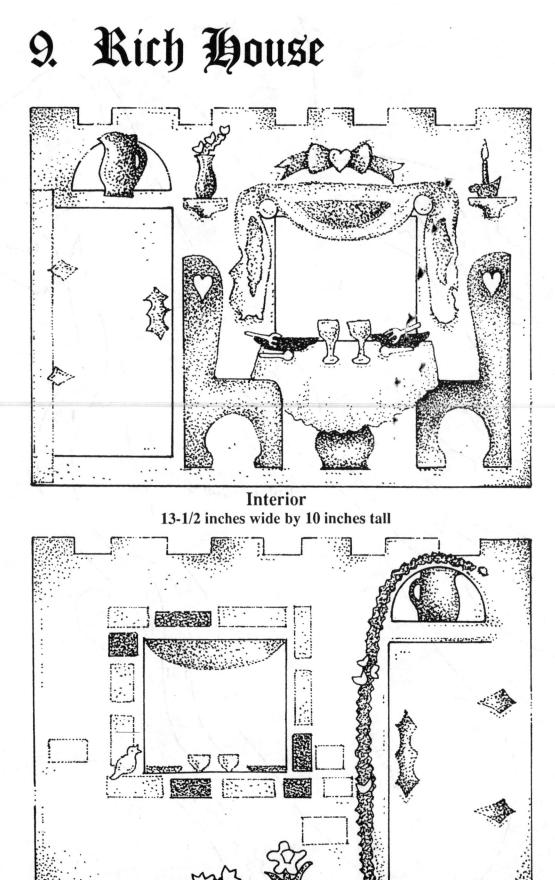

Interior
13-1/2 inches wide by 10 inches tall

Exterior

Rich House

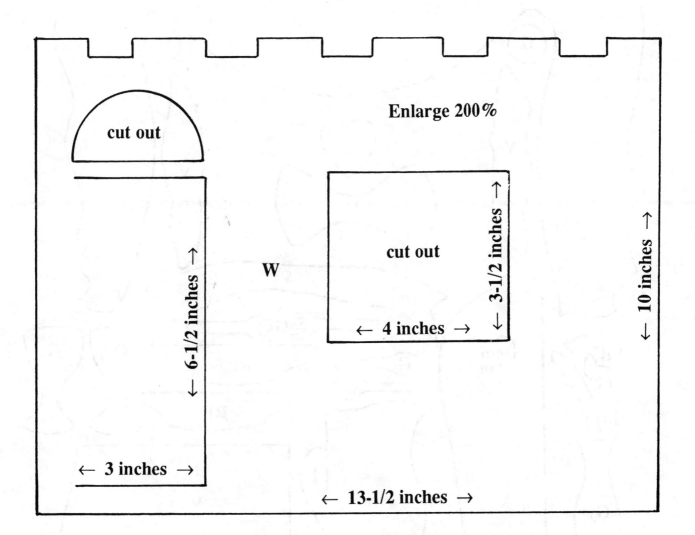

cut out

Enlarge 200%

cut out

← 3-1/2 inches →

← 4 inches →

← 6-1/2 inches →

W

← 10 inches →

← 3 inches →

← 13-1/2 inches →

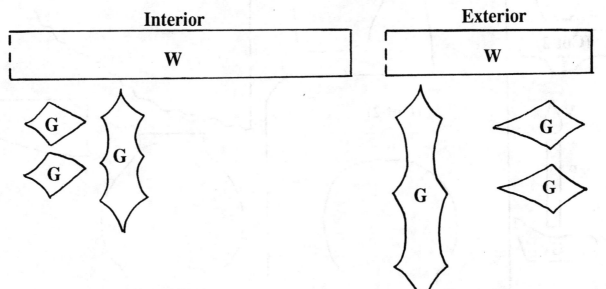

Interior

W

Exterior

W

G

G

G

G

G

G

Detail patterns to interior of Rich House

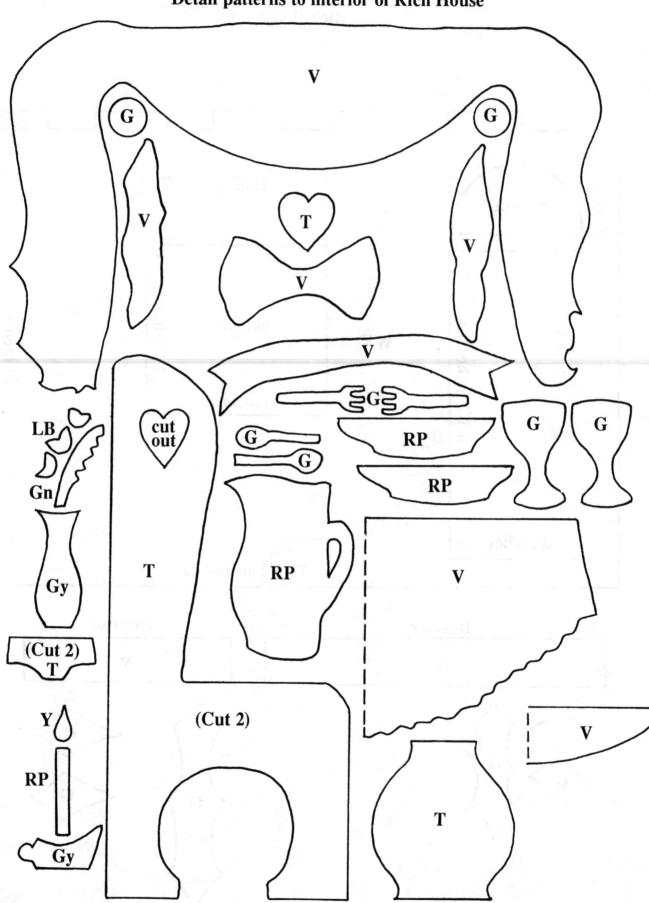

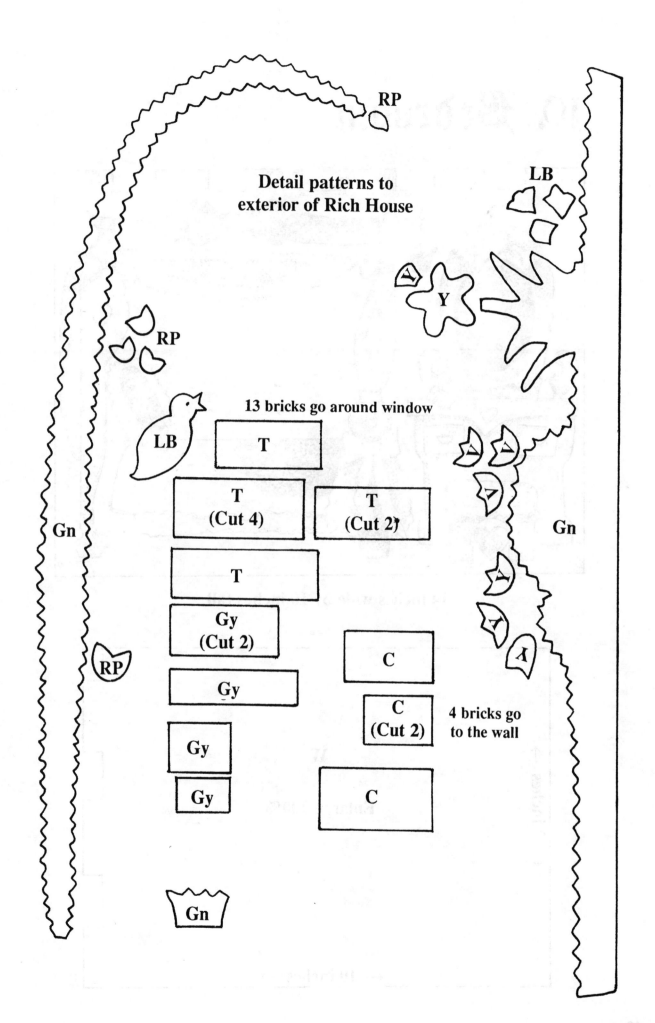

Detail patterns to exterior of Rich House

RP

LB

Y

RP

13 bricks go around window

LB

T

T (Cut 4)

T (Cut 2)

T

Gn

Gy (Cut 2)

Gy

C

RP

Gy

C (Cut 2)

4 bricks go to the wall

Gy

Gn

C

10. Bedroom

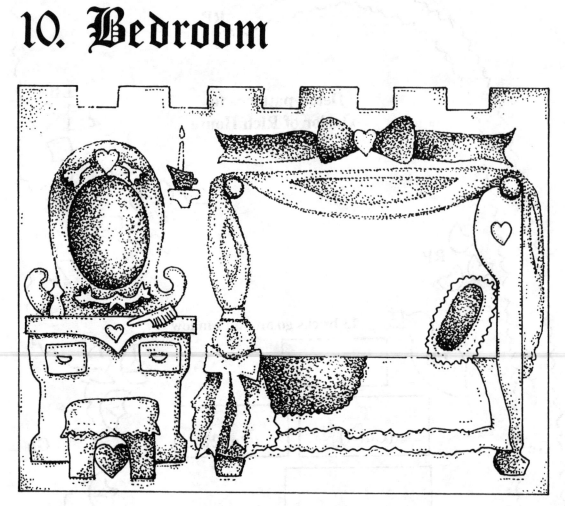

14 inches wide by 10 inches tall

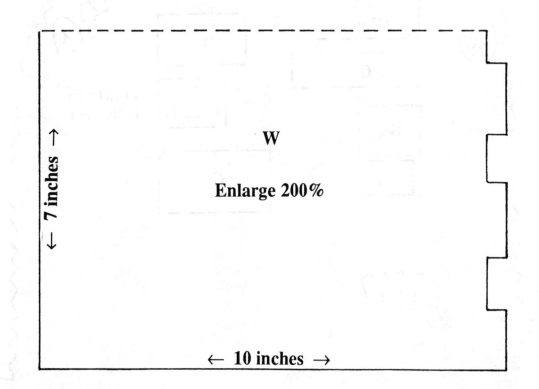

← 7 inches →

W

Enlarge 200%

← 10 inches →

Bedroom

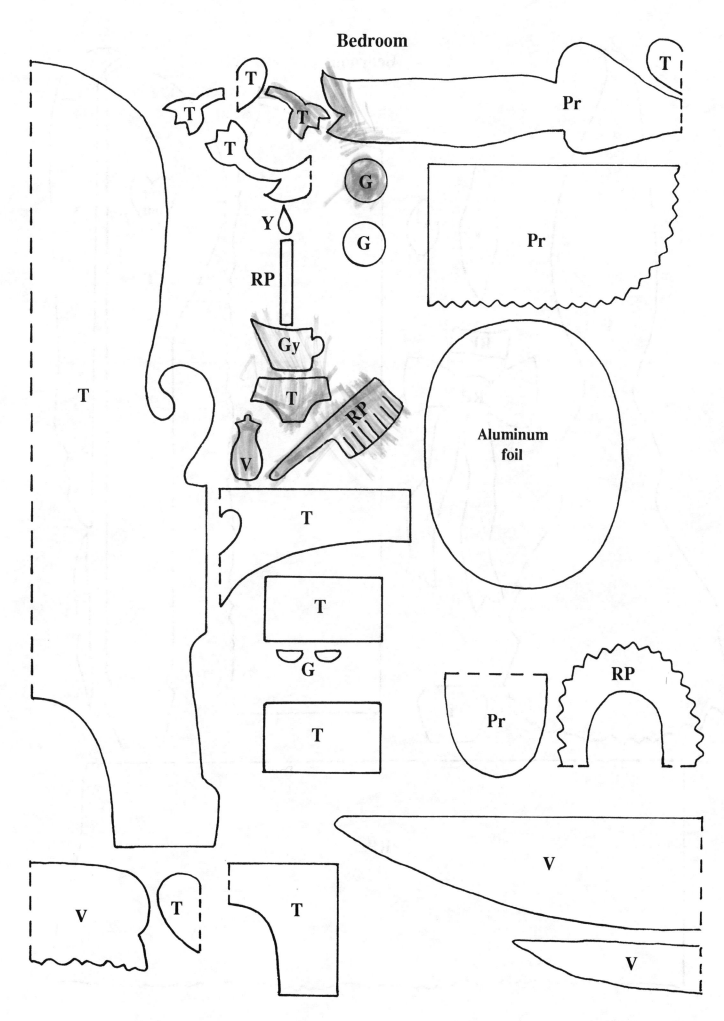

Bedroom

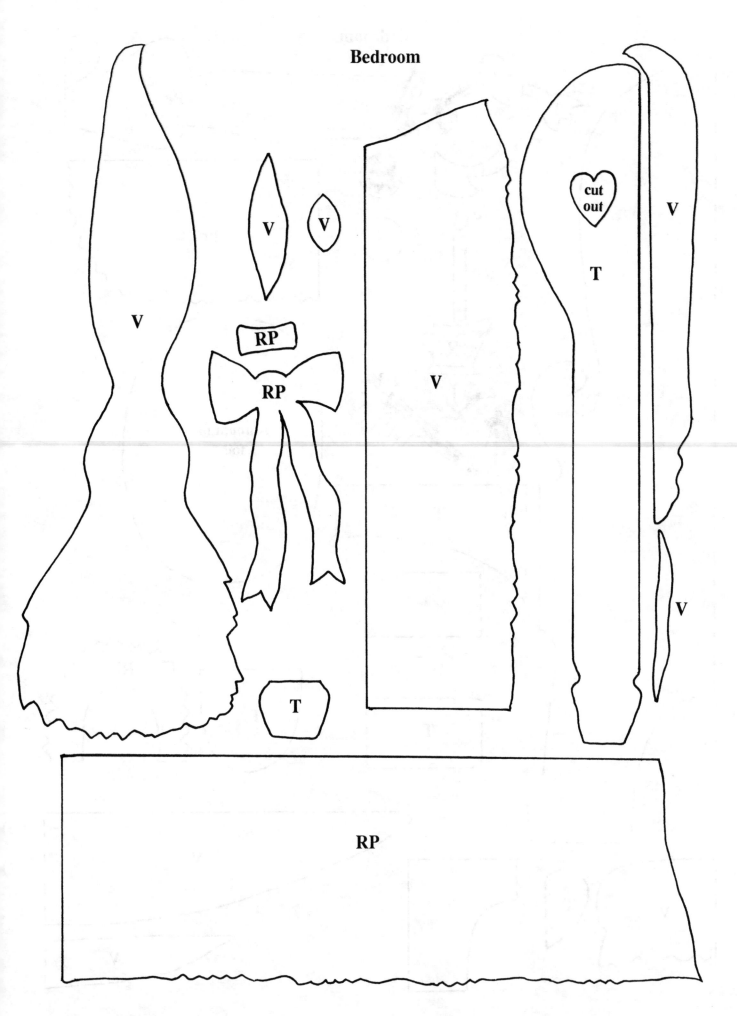

42

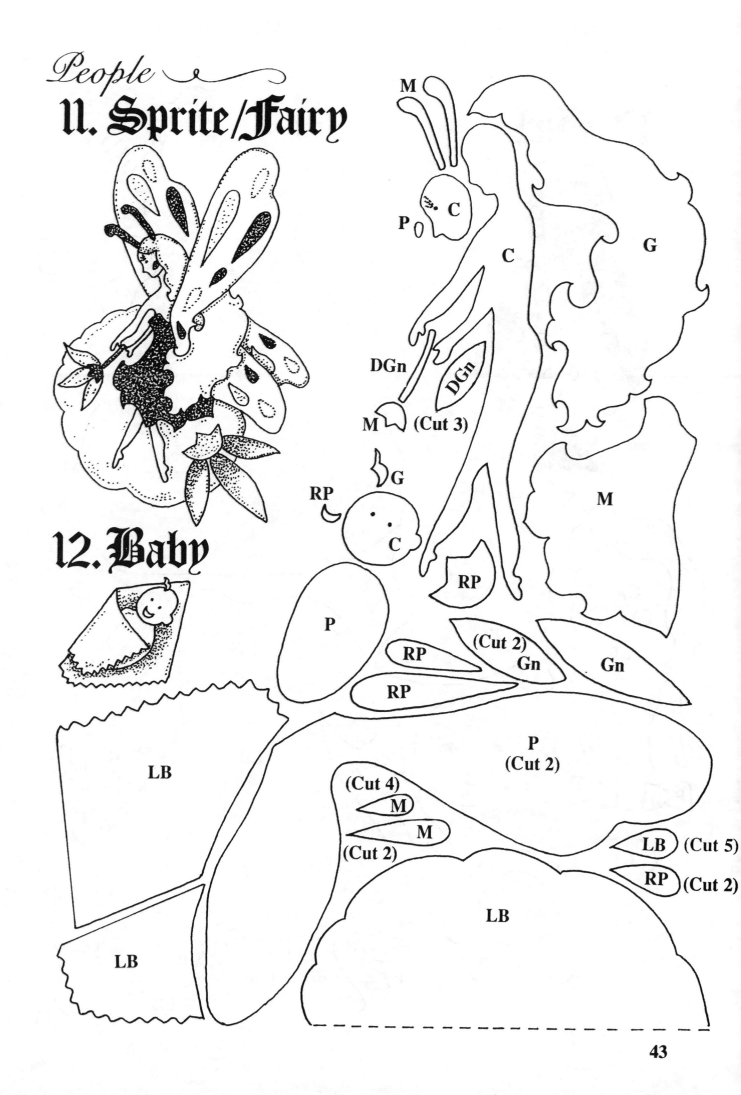

People

11. Sprite/Fairy

12. Baby

M

P 0 · C

C

G

DGn

DGn

M (Cut 3)

M

RP

G

C

RP

P

RP

(Cut 2)

Gn

Gn

RP

P
(Cut 2)

(Cut 4)

M

M

LB

LB (Cut 5)

(Cut 2)

RP (Cut 2)

LB

LB

13. Girl

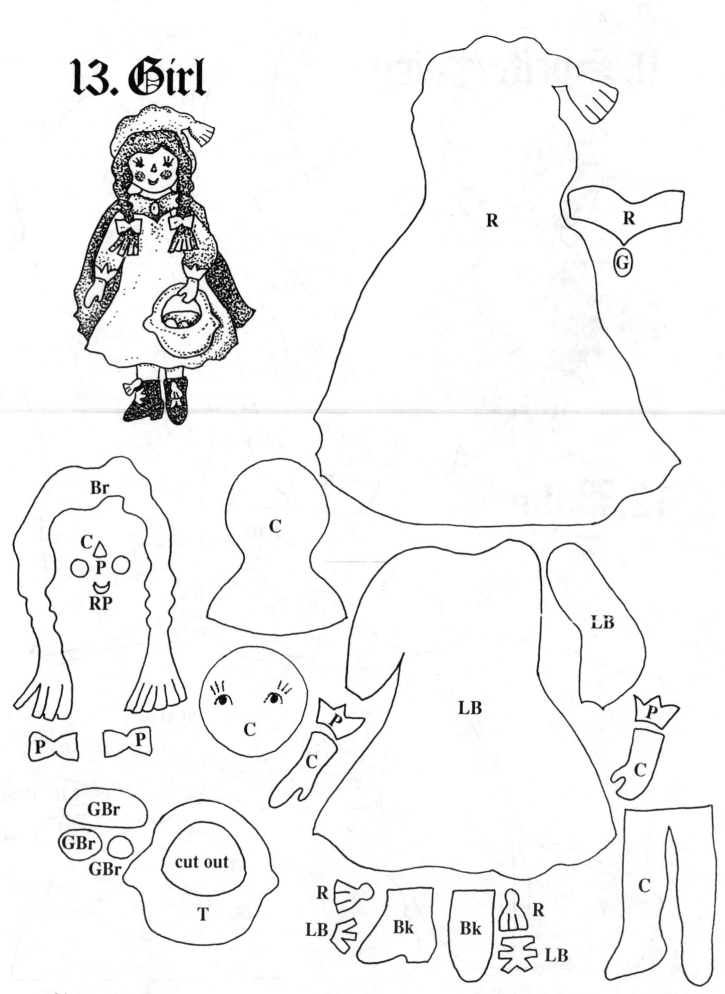

R

R

G

Br

C △
○ P ○
RP

C

C

LB

LB

LB

P

C

P

C

P

P

GBr

GBr

GBr

cut out

T

R

LB

Bk

Bk

R

LB

C

14. Woman

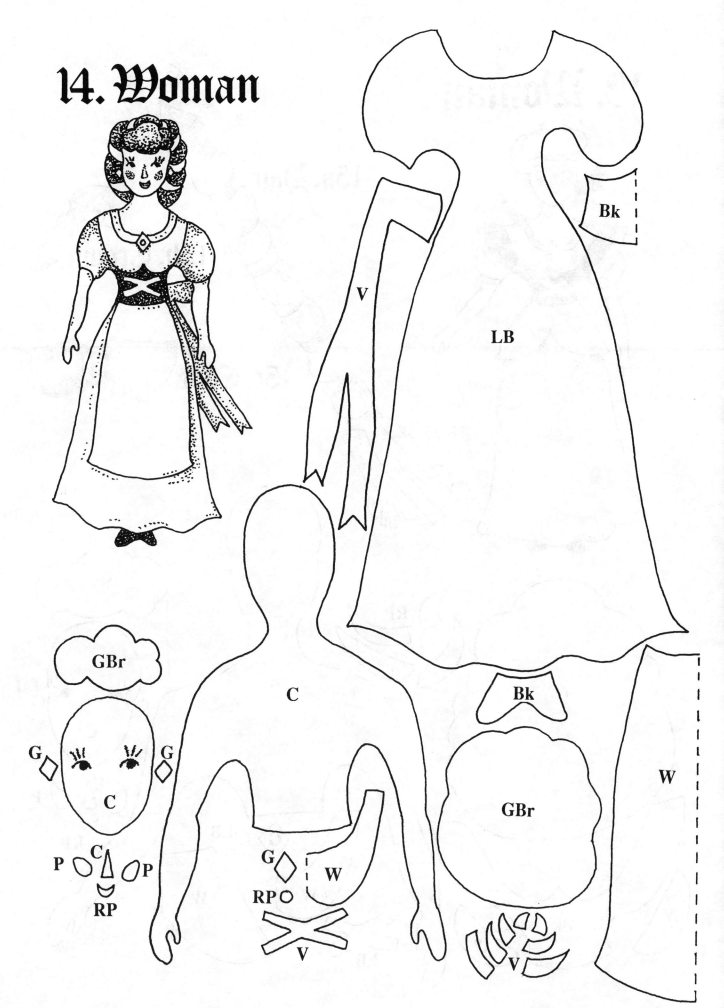

15. Woman

15a. Hair

15b. Crown

15c. Cape

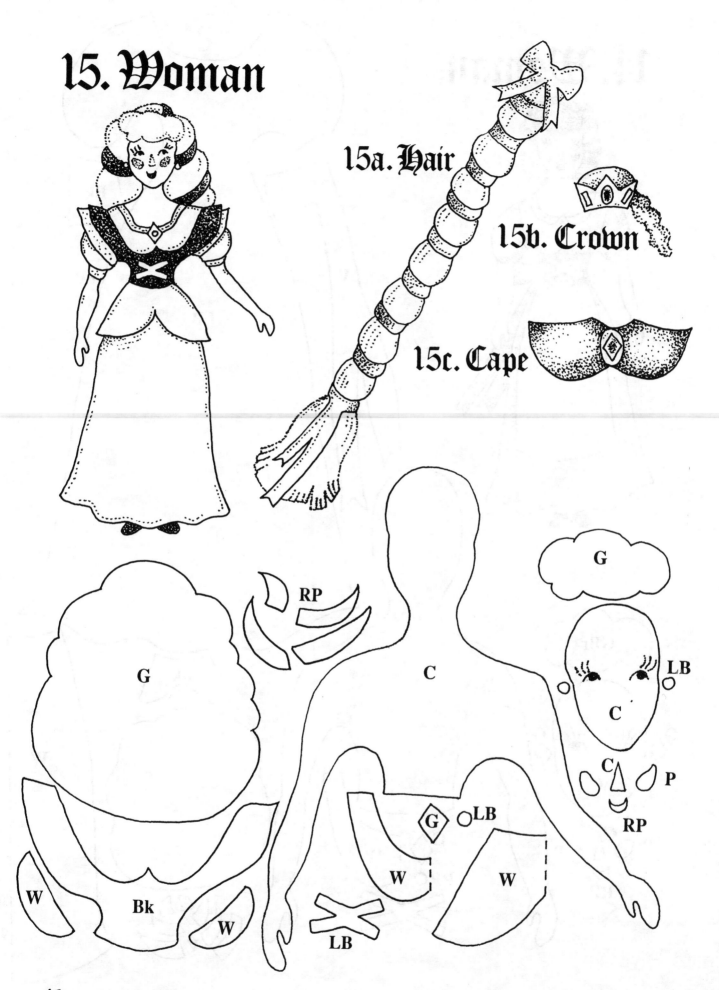

15. Woman

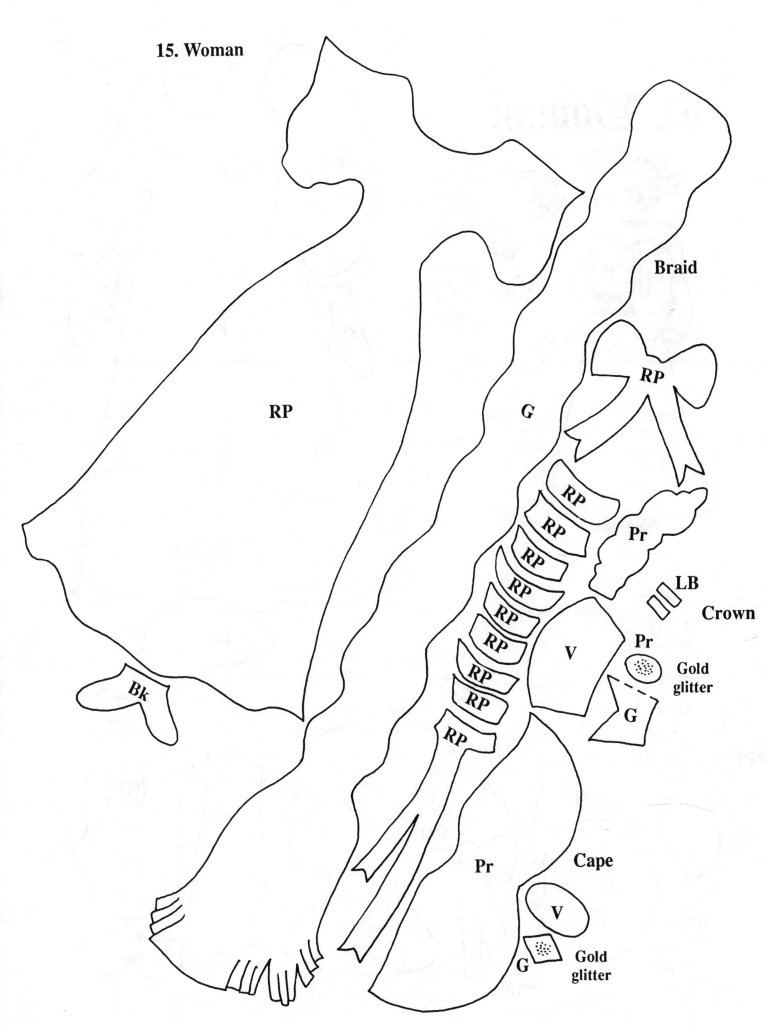

Braid

RP

RP

G

RP

RP

RP

Pr

RP

RP

LB

Crown

RP

RP

V

Pr

RP

Gold glitter

RP

Bk

RP

G

RP

RP

Pr

Cape

V

G

Gold glitter

16. Woman

16a. Cap

17. Woman

C

C

C

R

Bk

Gy

C

RB

C

RB
(Cut 6)

Bk

RP

R

RB

RB

18. Man

18a. Crown

18b. Trousers

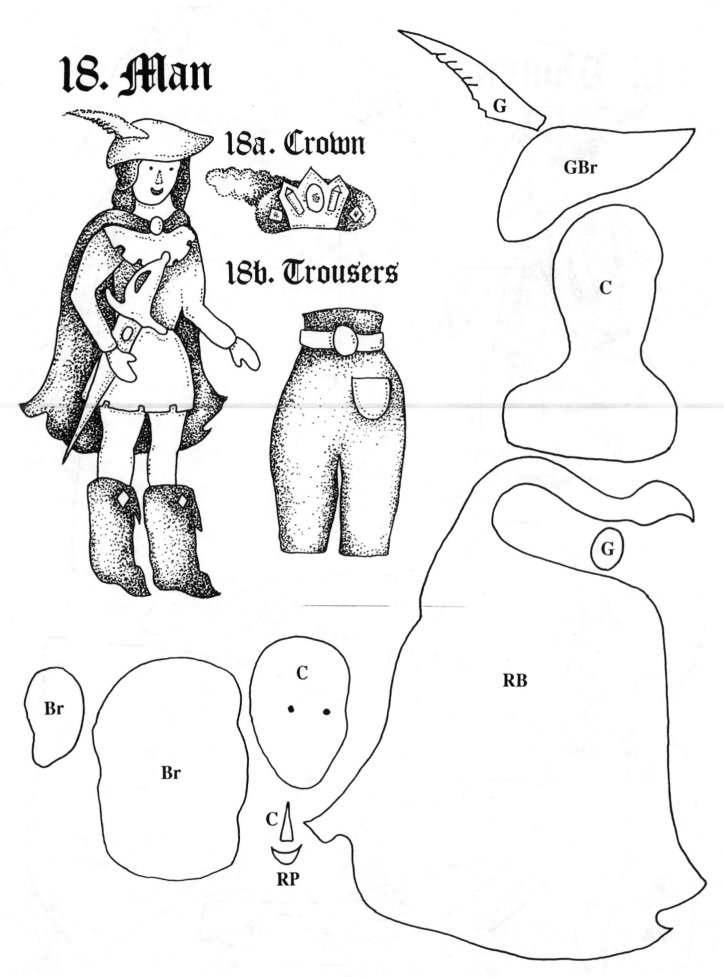

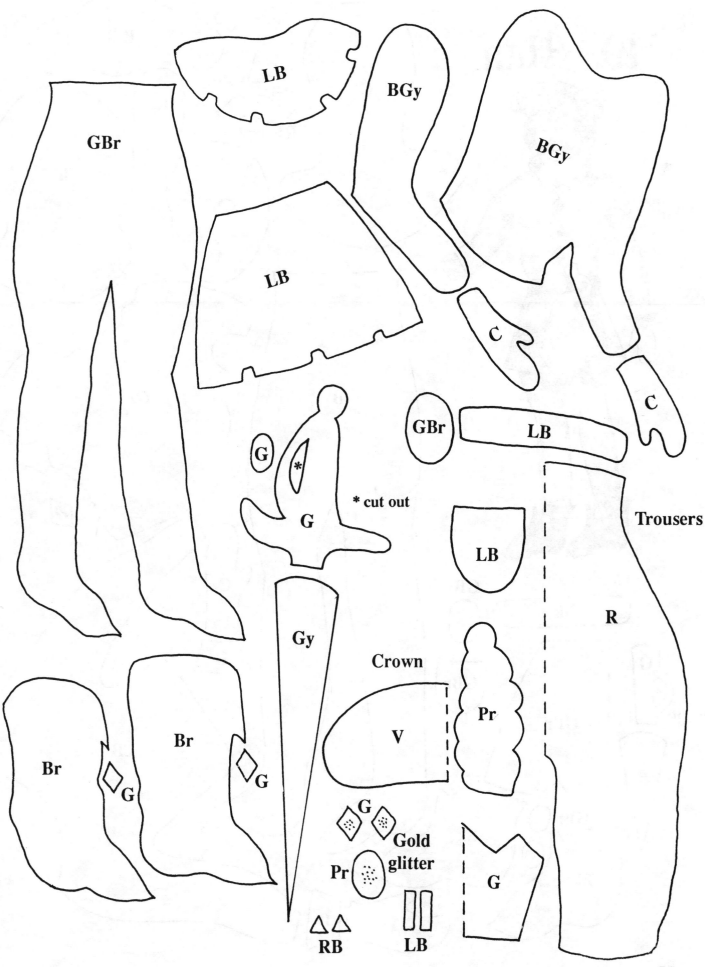

GBr

LB

BGy

BGy

LB

C

GBr

LB

C

G

*

* cut out

G

Trousers

LB

R

Gy

Crown

Pr

V

Br

Br

G

G

G

Gold glitter

Pr

G

RB

LB

51

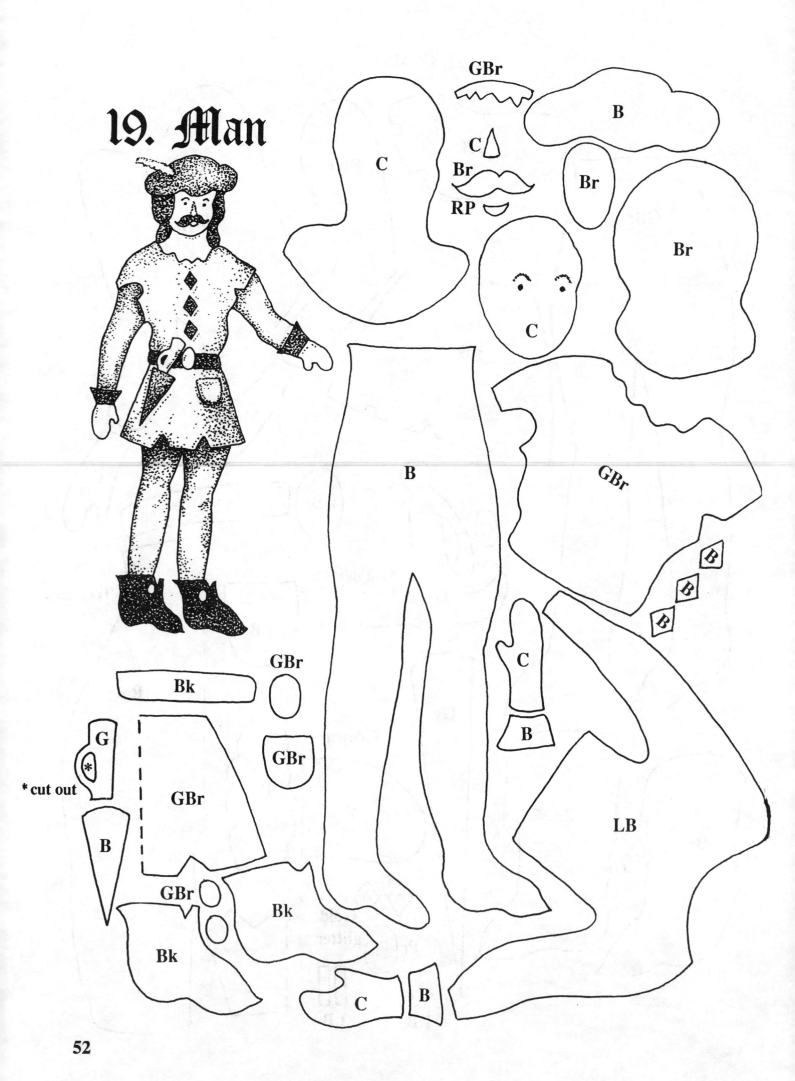

19. Man

GBr

C

B

C

Br

Br

Br

RP

C

C

B

GBr

B

B

B

B

C

B

GBr

Bk

GBr

GBr

G

* cut out

GBr

B

GBr

Bk

Bk

C

B

LB

52

20. Man

20a. Crown

21. Gingerbread Man

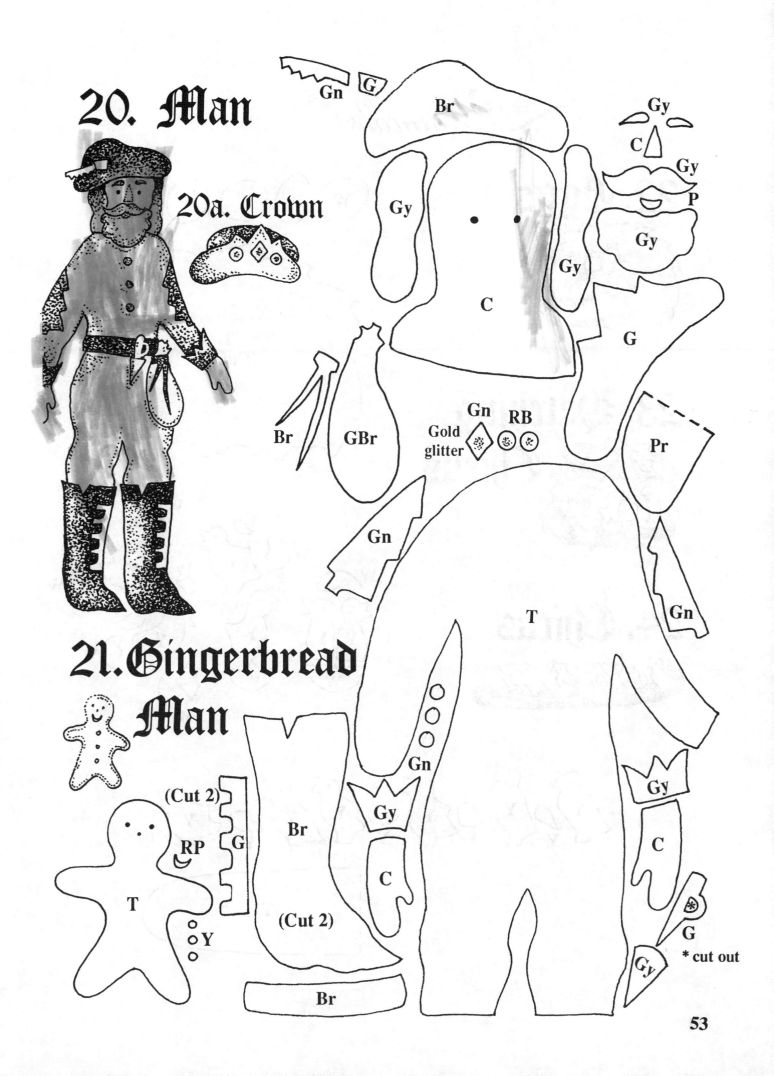

Gn G

Br

Gy Gy

Br

GBr

Gn RB
Gold glitter

Gn

Gy

Gy C

Gy P

Gy

G

Pr

Gn

T

Gn

Gy

C

G

* cut out

Gy

(Cut 2)

RP G Br

T

Y

(Cut 2)

Br

22. Eggs

23. Hatching Chicks

24. Chicks

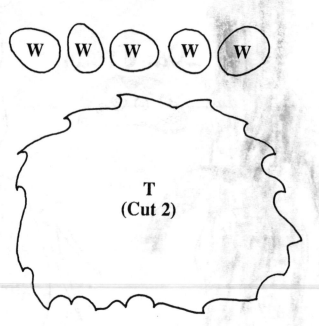

W W W W W

T
(Cut 2)

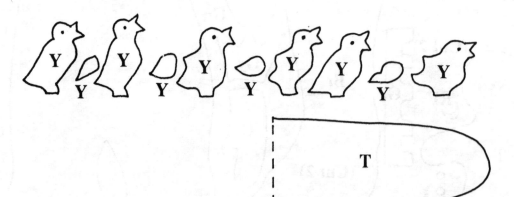

T

54

25. Dog

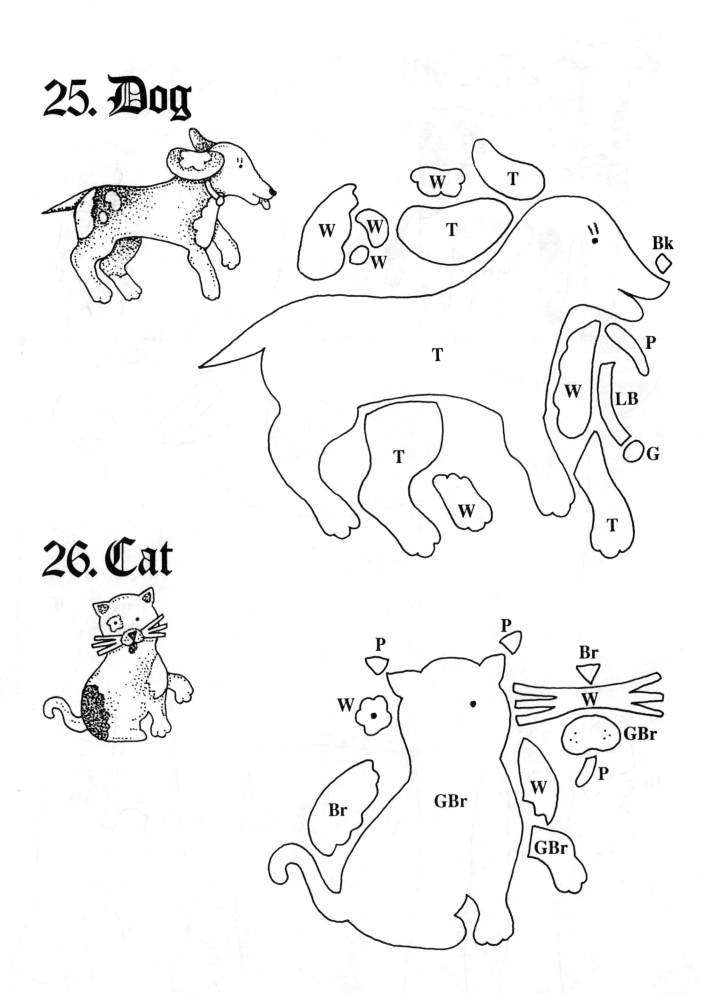

26. Cat

27. Cow

Bk

T

Bk

W

T

Bk

P

G

R

W

Bk

Bk

Bk

Bk

Bk

Bk

W

P

T

56

28. Frog

29. Hen

30. Rooster

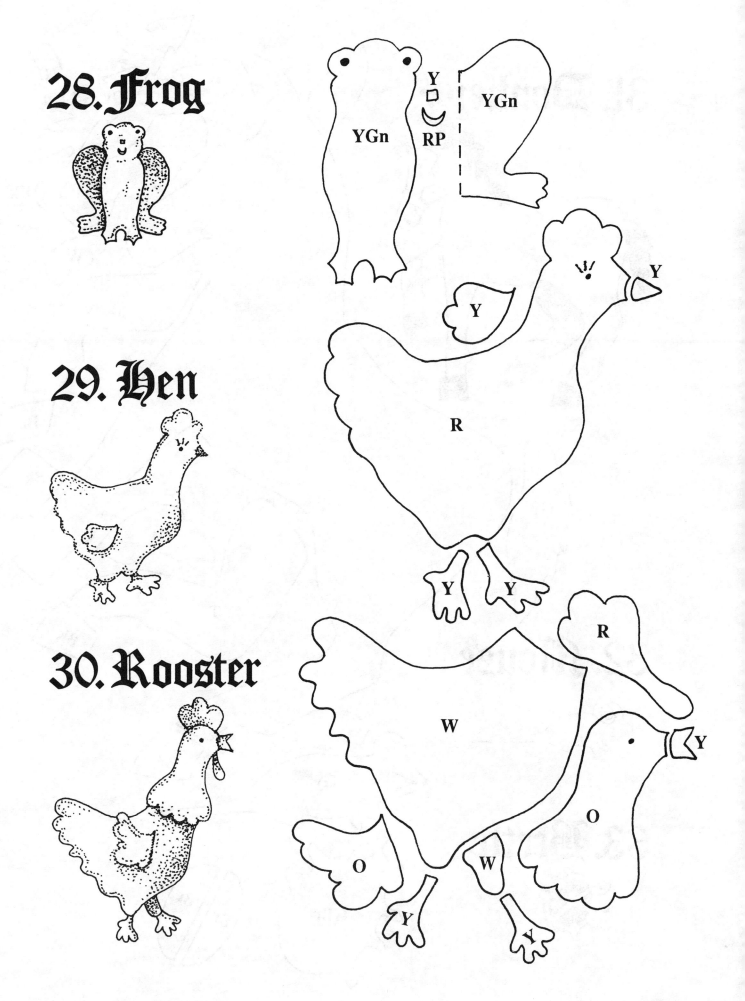

31. Donkey

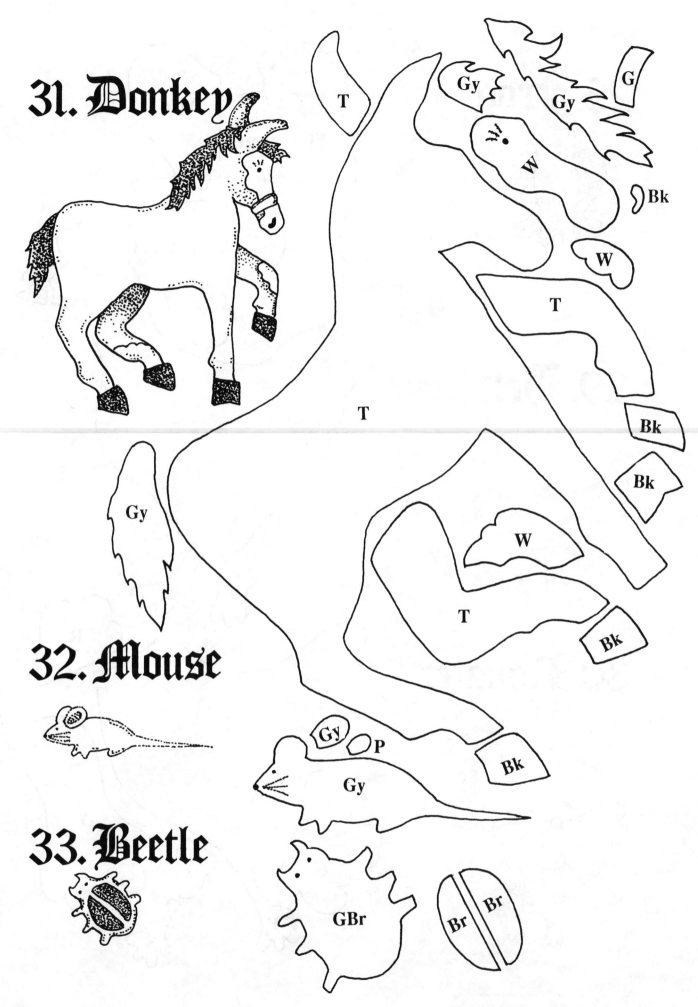

32. Mouse

33. Beetle

34. Fox

GBr

W

GBr

GBr

RP

W

GBr

35. Wolf/
Coyote

Gy

Gy

RP

Bk

W

Gy

Gy

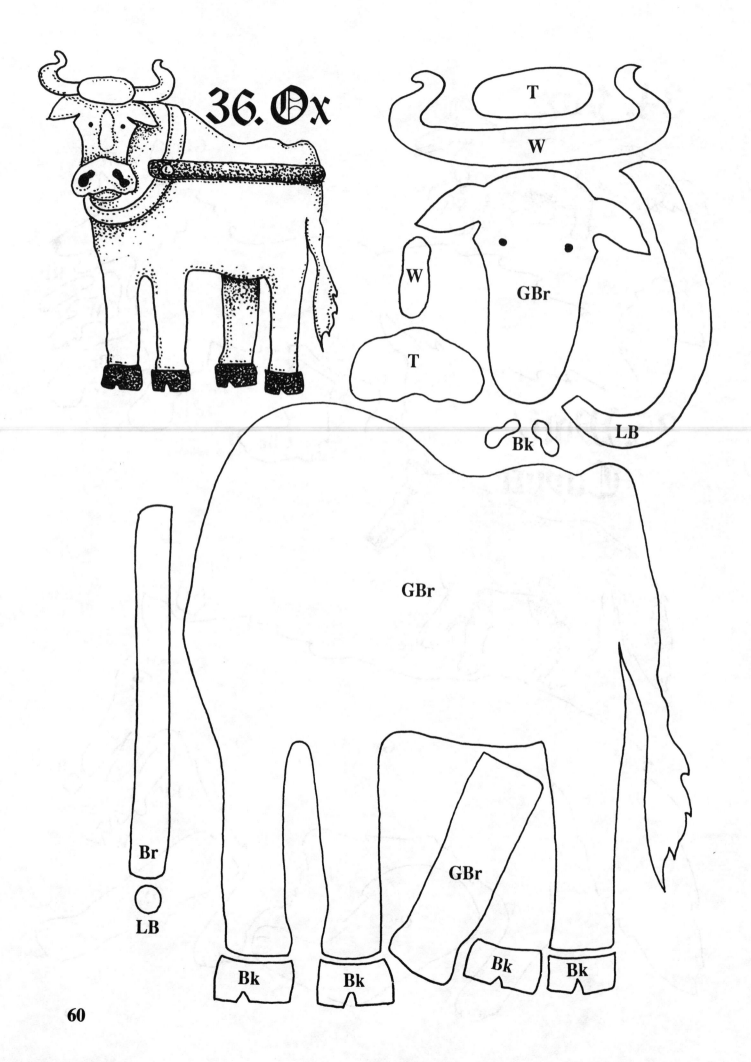

36. Ox

60

37. Pig

38. Tiger

39. Monkey

40. Deer

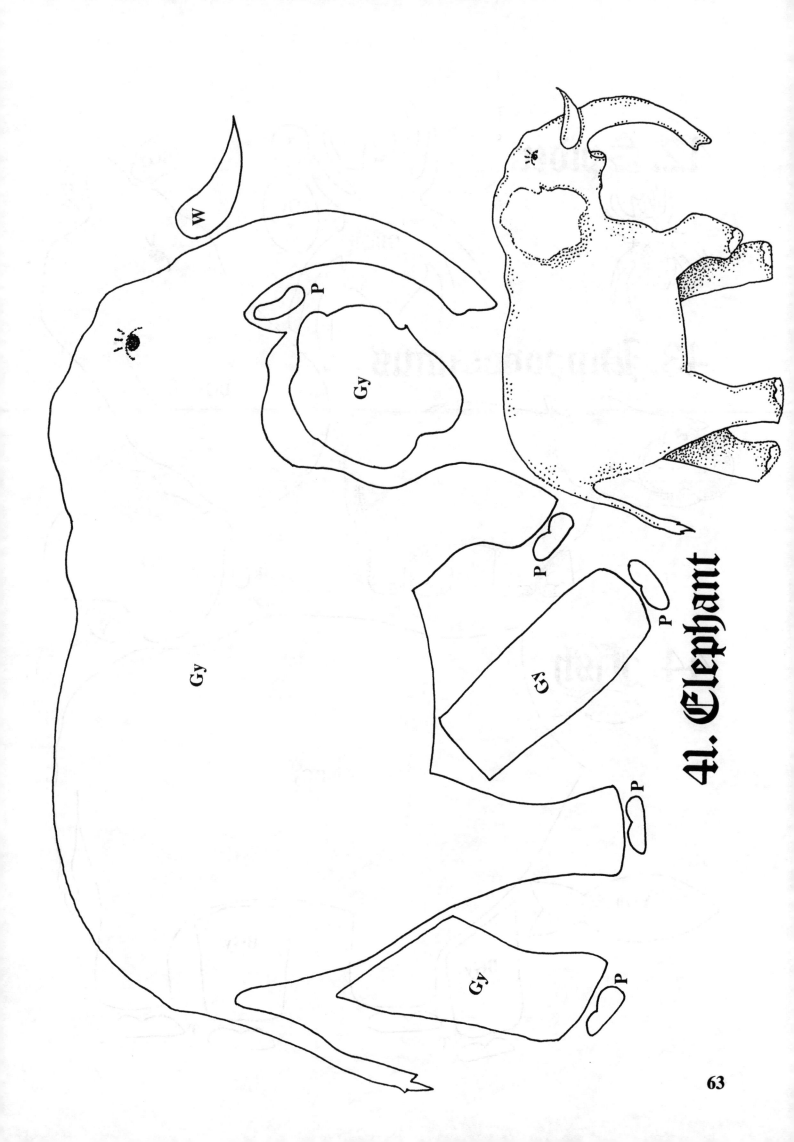

W

P

Gy

Gy

P

Gy

P

P

Gy

P

41. Elephant

42. Spider

43. Hippopotamus

44. Fish

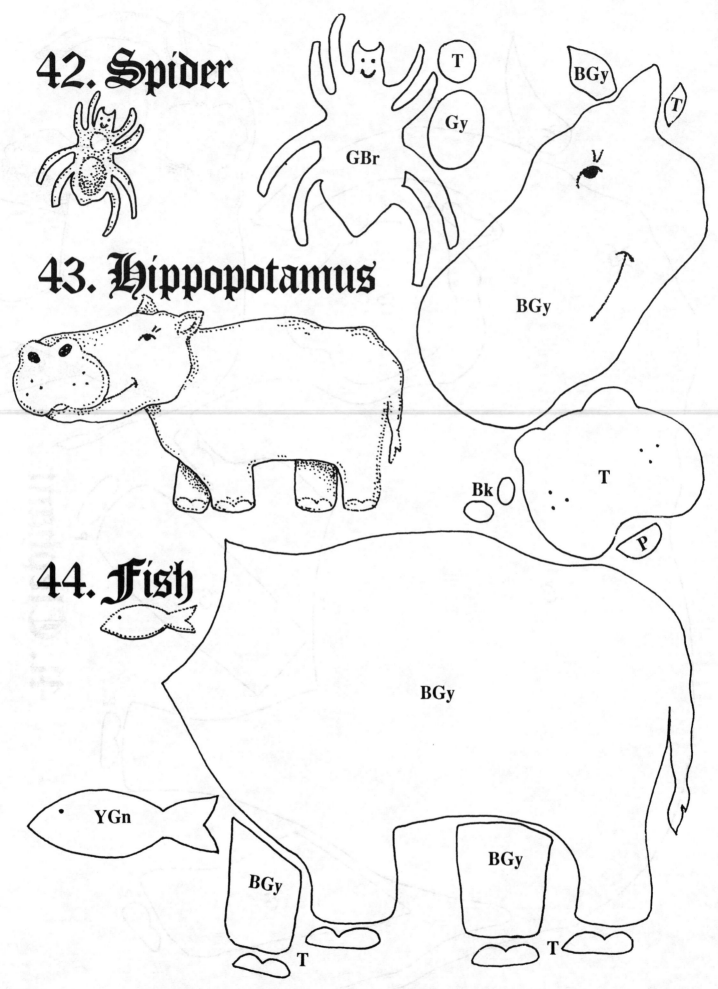

45. Stile

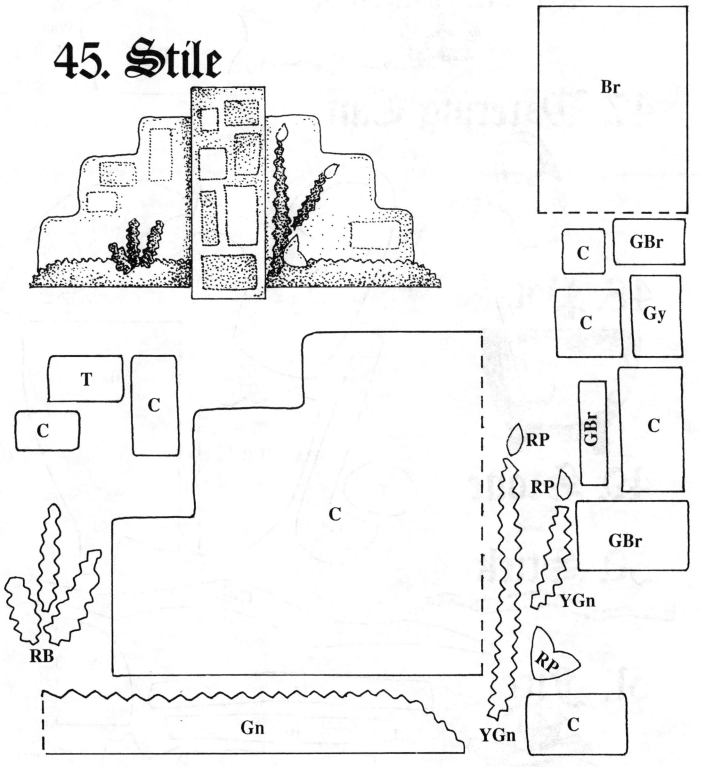

46. Bread

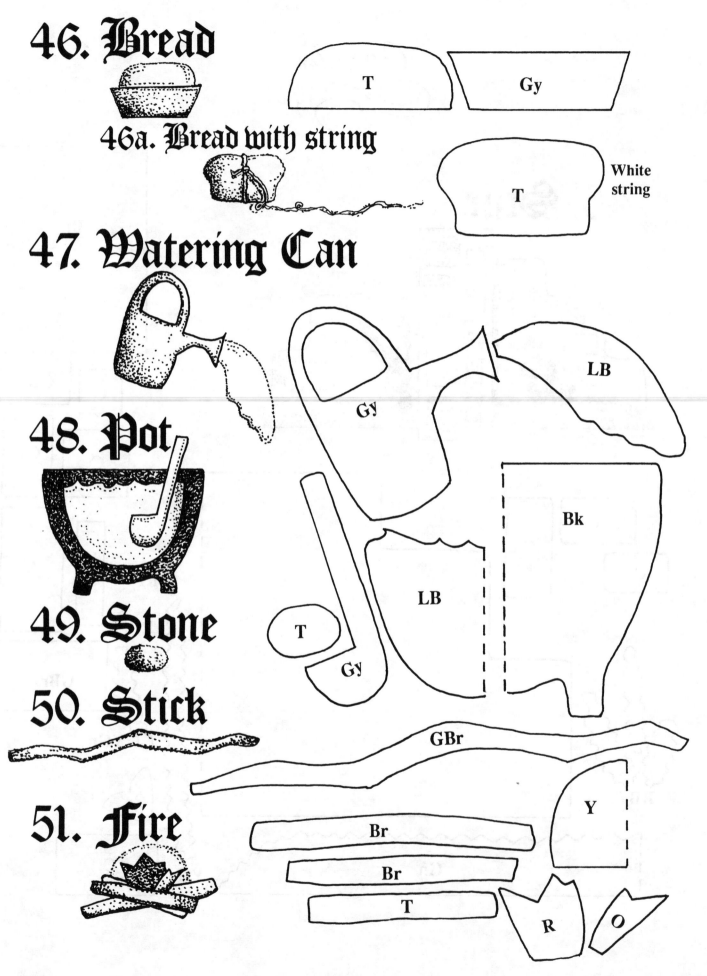

46a. Bread with string

T Gy

T White string

47. Watering Can

Gy LB

Bk

LB

T Gy

48. Pot

49. Stone

50. Stick

GBr

51. Fire

Y

Br

Br

T

R O

66

52. Hay

53. Rake

54. Pail

55. Bowl

56. Sausage

57. Sign

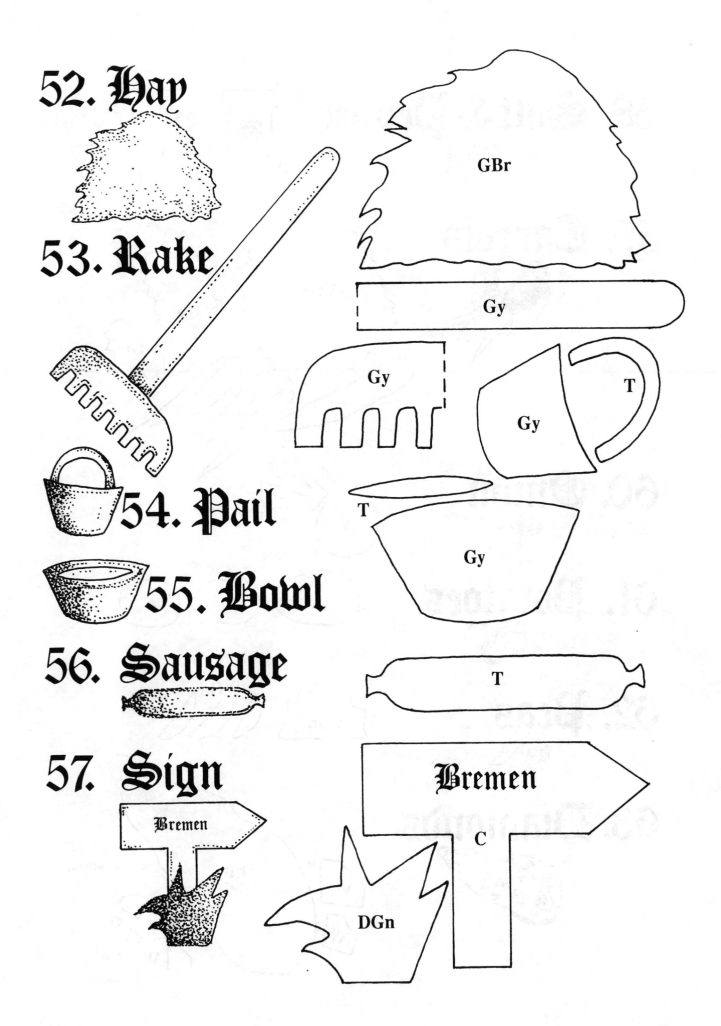

GBr

Gy

Gy

T

Gy

T

Gy

T

Bremen

Bremen

C

DGn

67

58. Salt & Pepper

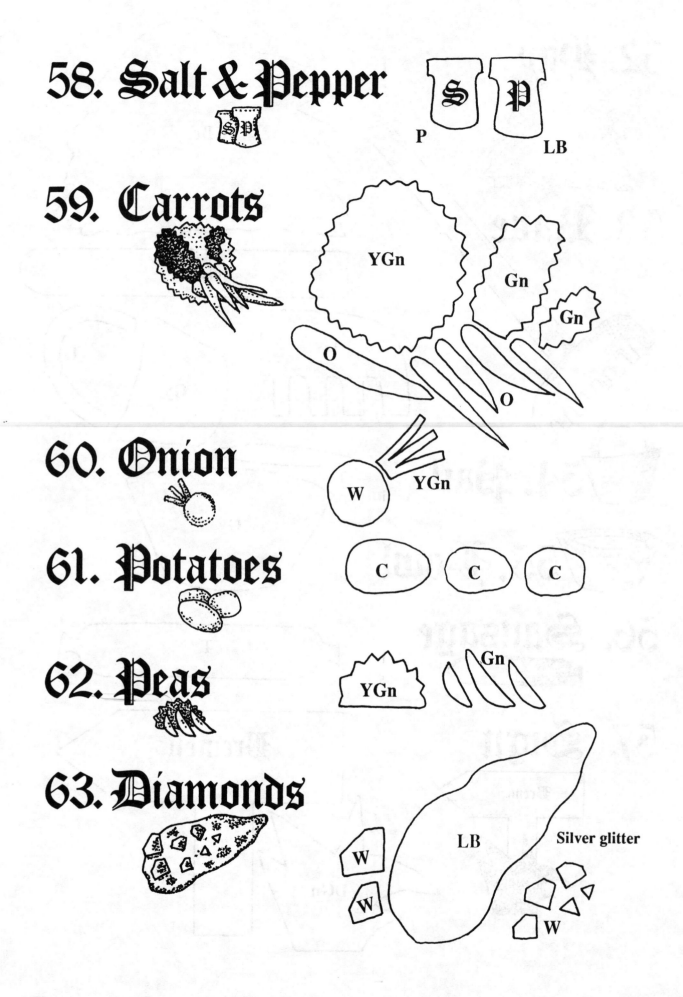

P

LB

59. Carrots

YGn

Gn

Gn

O

O

60. Onion

W

YGn

61. Potatoes

C   C   C

62. Peas

YGn   Gn

63. Diamonds

W

W

LB

Silver glitter

W

64. Spinning Wheel

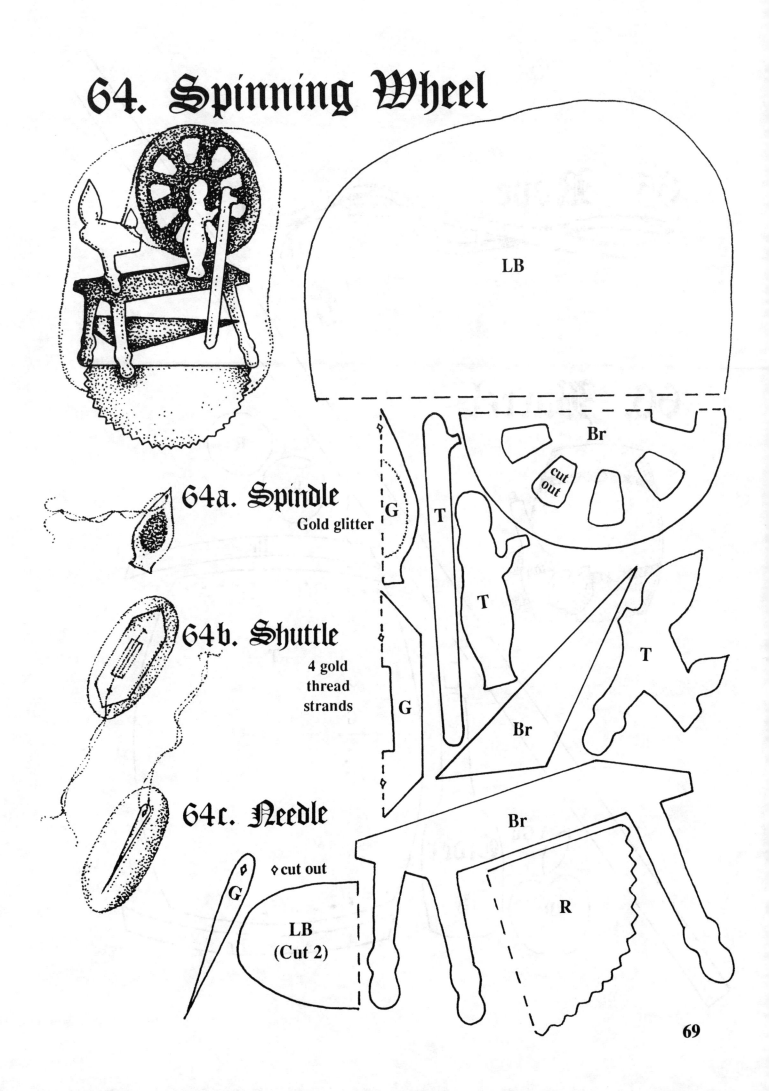

64a. Spindle

Gold glitter

64b. Shuttle

4 gold
thread
strands

64c. Needle

LB

Br

cut
out

G

T

T

T

G

G

Br

Br

R

◊ cut out

G

LB
(Cut 2)

65. Rope

66. Barrel

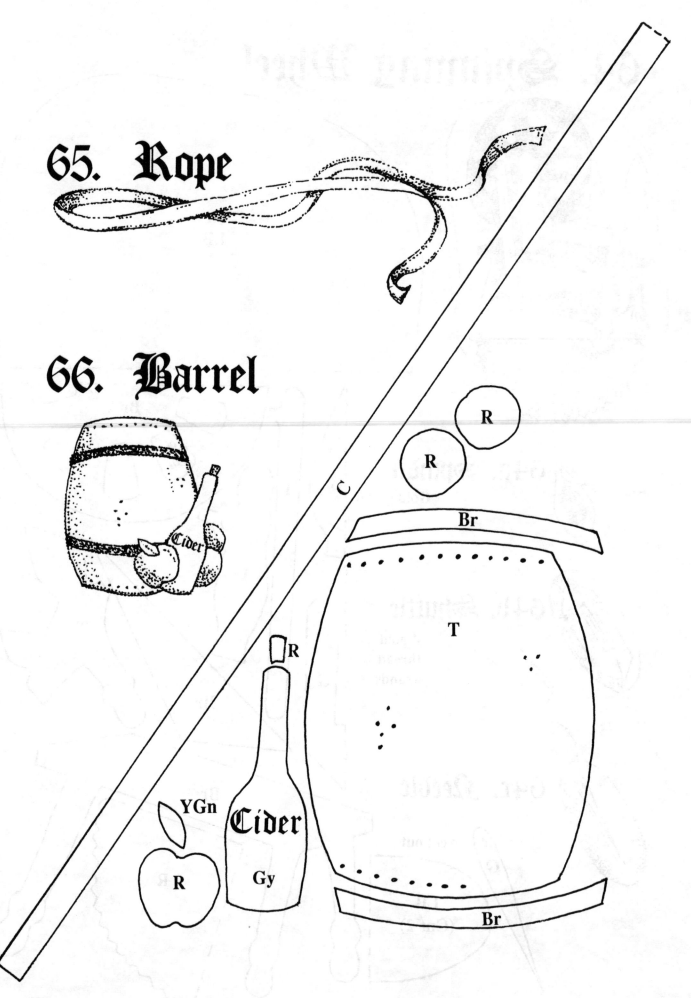

C

R

R

Br

T

R

YGn

Cider

R

Gy

Br

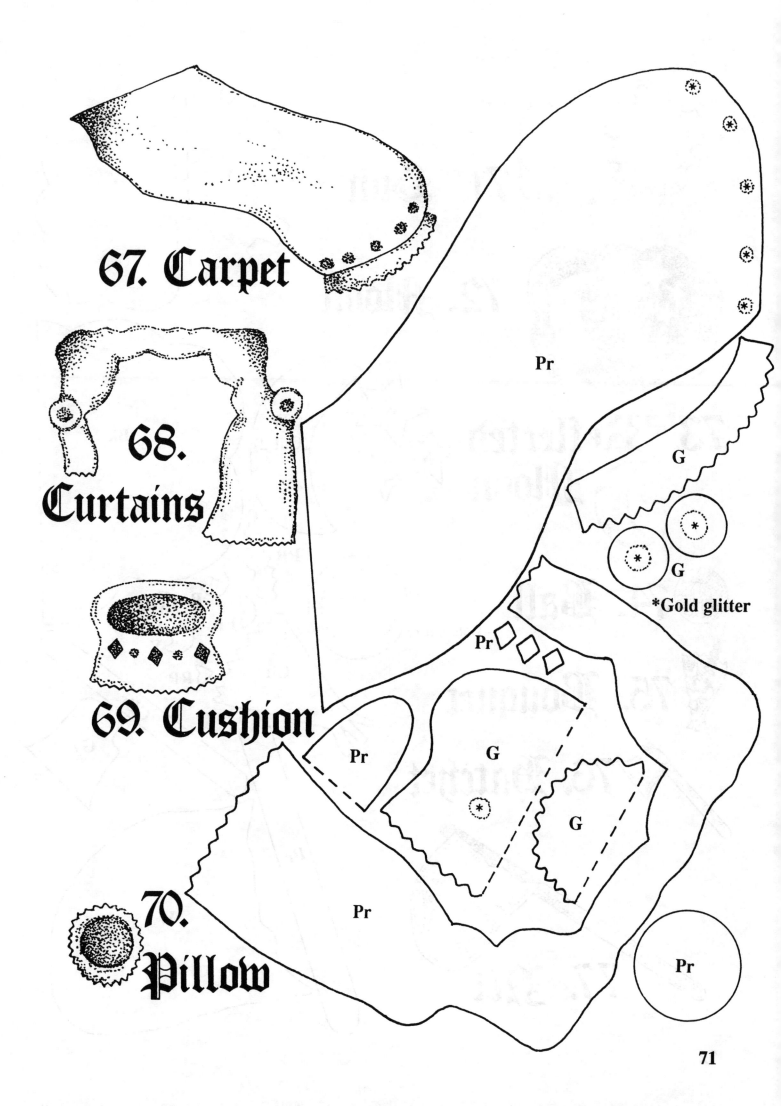

67. Carpet

68. Curtains

69. Cushion

70. Pillow

Pr

G

G

*Gold glitter

Pr

G

Pr

Pr

G

Pr

Pr

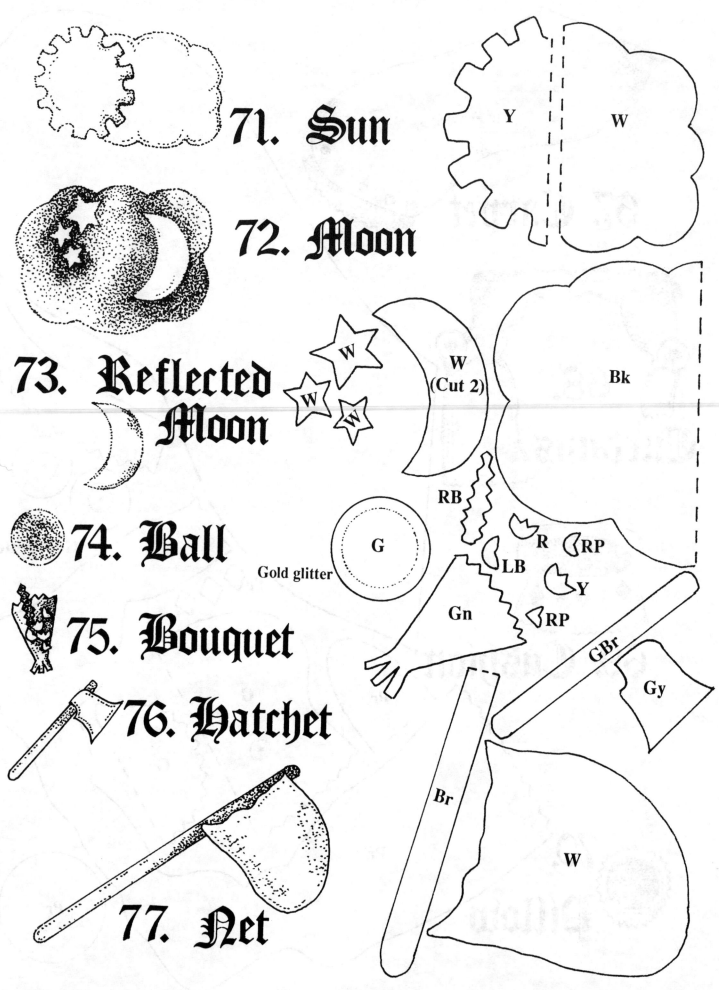

71. Sun

72. Moon

73. Reflected Moon

74. Ball

75. Bouquet

76. Hatchet

77. Net

Y

W

W
(Cut 2)

Bk

W

W

W

RB

G

Gold glitter

LB

R

RP

Y

RP

Gn

GBr

Gy

Br

W

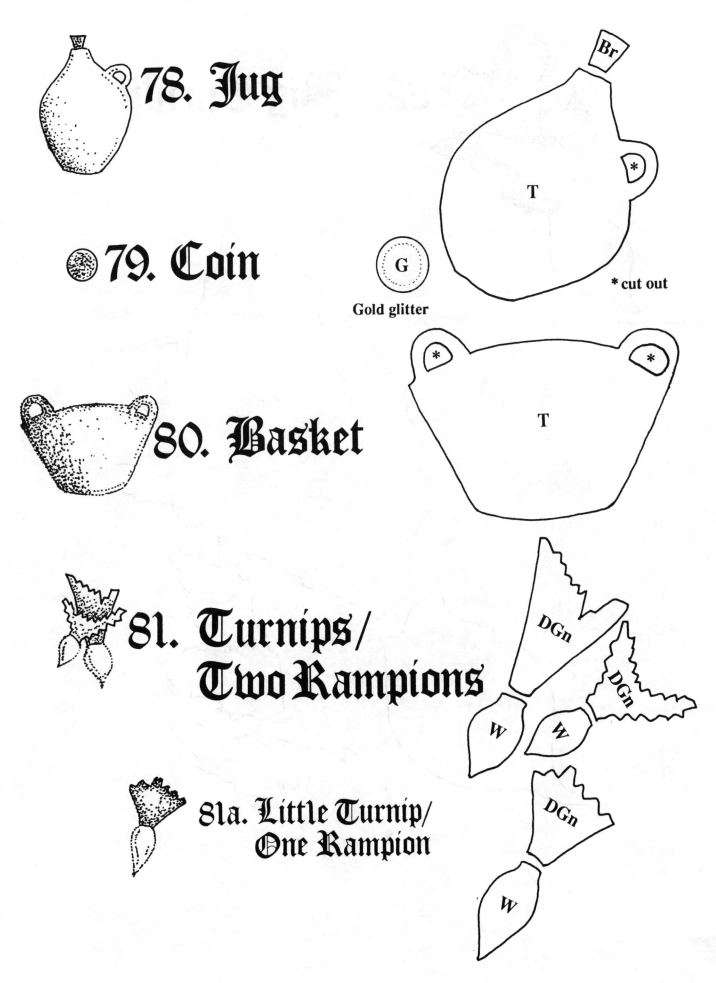

78. Jug

79. Coin

G
Gold glitter

T

Br

T

* cut out

80. Basket

81. Turnips/ Two Rampions

DGn

DGn

W   W

81a. Little Turnip/ One Rampion

DGn

W

82. Big Turnip

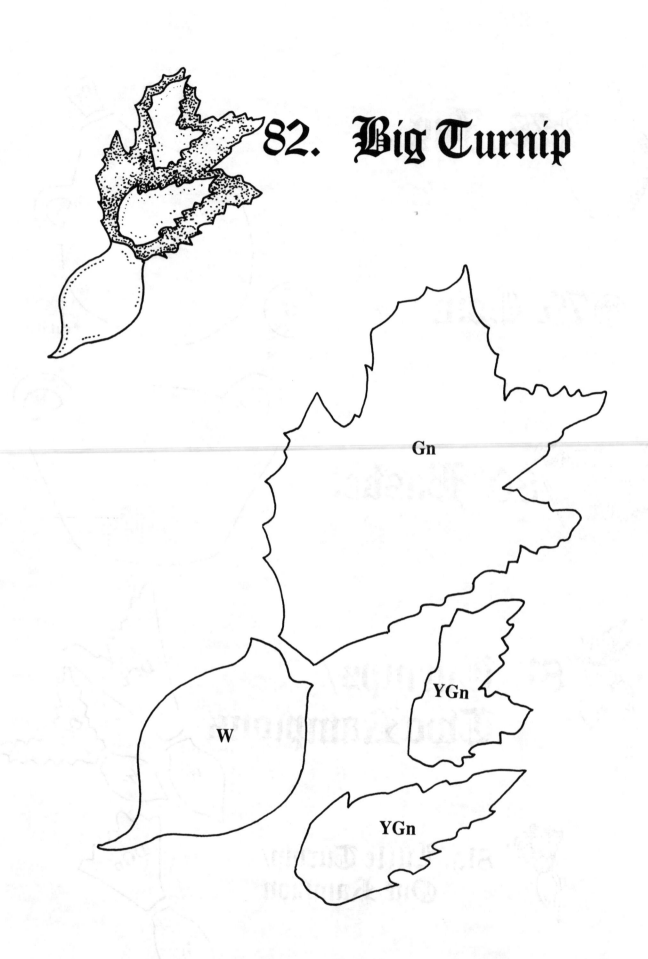

II

Eighteen Classic Tales

Introduction

"King of the Forest," a folktale collected in China, is an easy one for a beginning storyteller to present. The plot proceeds in a simple sequence of events, so felt figures are put onto the flannelboard and later removed after very little shifting of figures from one spot to another on the board.

Before presenting the story, look through library books about China with the children to learn which wild animals live in modern China. Children may know that pandas live there, but they are often surprised to discover that monkeys, deer, and other animals that are usually associated with Africa also live in China. Read together a book about elephants to find out where elephants are living today, and locate their current homelands and China on a world map.

Set-Up Instructions

Set up the following figure near the bottom center of flannelboard:

    6. Forest

Set up figures on the table, left to right:

    34. Fox

    38. Tiger

    39. Monkey

    40. Deer

    41. Elephant

Read Aloud

SCRIPT	FLANNELBOARD
One day Fox was out in the forest, looking for food. He walked carefully all around, looking to the left and looking to the right, sniffing to the left and sniffing to the right. He walked forward, and he looked forward, looking far ahead of him for something to eat. The one place he did not look was behind him.	**Put up FOX on left.** **Move FOX to left edge of FOREST.**
Behind the Fox was Tiger, who was out hunting for food. Tiger saw something good to eat. He ran forward, and he jumped right on top of Fox, holding him down under his sharp and powerful claws.	**Put up TIGER behind FOX.** **Move TIGER onto FOX.**
Tiger opened his mouth wide, and he moved toward Fox with all his teeth gleaming in the sun. But before he could clamp his jaws shut, Fox said in a loud voice, "How dare you?"	
Tiger was so surprised that he just stood there with his mouth still hanging open. He didn't say anything.	
Fox continued, "How dare you jump onto the King of the Forest?"	
Tiger looked all around and said, "Where is the King of the Forest? Who is the King of the Forest?"	**Move TIGER slightly to left.**
Fox replied, "Well, I am, of course. Didn't you know that all the animals chose me to be king? They have so much respect for their new king that whenever they see me coming, they jump back out of my way and let me pass by."	
Tiger said, "I don't believe you. A little fuzzy creature like you? You're just a ball of fluff, and half of that is nothing but tail. Nobody would run away at the sight of you."	
Fox answered, "Then I'll prove it to you. Follow me as I walk through the forest."	
So Tiger got down off Fox's back, and the two animals began to walk in a straight line through the forest. They hadn't gone very far when they ran across a monkey sitting on a rock by a tall tree. As soon as Monkey saw who was walking toward her through the forest, she climbed straight up a tree and took off through the treetops just as fast as she could go.	**Move TIGER to left.** **Put up MONKEY on rock.** **Move MONKEY to treetop.**

Fox and Tiger walked on and on, deeper into the forest. As they entered a clearing between the trees, they came upon a deer grazing in the grass. The deer looked over his shoulder, and as soon as he saw who was approaching him, he ran deep into the forest, zig-zagging between the trees.

Put up DEER to right of rock.

Take down DEER.

Tiger and Fox continued to walk through the forest. When they got near the watering hole, they saw an elephant about to get a drink of water. When she lowered her head to drink, she looked around and saw who was coming up behind her. So she took off down the trail just as fast as she could go.

Put up ELEPHANT at right.

Take down ELEPHANT.

Tiger just shook his head in wonder. He said, "You were right, Fox. When the animals saw you, they ran away. You really must be the King of the Forest. I wouldn't dare to eat the King of the Forest." Tiger turned around and walked away.

Take down TIGER.

Fox walked on through the forest, looking for food. He walked carefully all around, looking to the left and looking to the right, sniffing to the left and sniffing to the right. And he looked behind him, too, just in case.

Move FOX to right of FOREST.

Follow-Up Activities

Questions for Discussion or Writing

1. In this story, Fox tricked Tiger. What tricks have people ever played on you? Why did you believe what they said? How do some advertisements on television trick people? Do you believe what you hear and see on television? Why or why not?

2. If Fox had not made up the story about being king, what do you think Tiger would have done? What else could Fox have done to escape from Tiger? If Fox had heard Tiger coming from a distance, what might Fox have done?

Game

King of All I See

With children seated facing you, read aloud:

In the story, Tiger noticed everything around him as he walked through the forest looking for clues that Fox was really king of the forest. In this game you must carefully look at everything around you to find clues that something has been changed.

First look for a few seconds at everything in this room: the furniture, the walls, even the people. I will ask one of you to be It and go outside the room while the group chooses one item to change inside the room. We might hang a picture upside down or move a piece of furniture.

The person who is It has fifteen seconds after coming back inside to guess what is different. If the person who is It guesses correctly before the fifteen seconds are up, he or she may choose the next one to be It. If the person who is It guesses incorrectly, I will choose who goes next.

All of you may give silent clues to the guesser by looking at the item changed, or you may give false clues by looking everywhere else.

Recommended Read-Aloud
Books on Related Topics

Books about Kings and Queens

Babbitt, Natalie. *Bub: Or the Very Best Thing.* New York: HarperCollins, 1994.

Courlander, Harold. *The King's Drum and Other African Stories.* New York: Harcourt, 1962.

Seuss, Dr. *Yertle the Turtle and Other Stories.* New York: Random House, 1958.

Stone Soup

Introduction

The trickster tale "Stone Soup" or "Soup from a Nail" is available in many printed versions. The setting and characters vary among these versions. Some stories have three soldiers walking home from a war, and others tell about a lone man or woman on the road. The story takes place in Sweden, Russia, France, or "a strange country." Although the ingredients of the soup vary from story to story, every version includes the trickster character or characters who make and eat a pot of soup.

Set-Up Instructions

Set up the following figure near the bottom of the flannelboard:

7. Cottage (exterior view)

Set up figures on the table, left to right:

18. Man [soldier character in this tale]

9. Rich House (exterior view)

14. Woman

49. Stone

48. Pot

51. Fire

58. Salt and Pepper

60. Onion

59. Carrots

61. Potatoes

62. Peas

46. Bread

78. Jug

Read Aloud

SCRIPT	FLANNELBOARD
Once there was a soldier who had served his king well for many years. Now he was on his way back home, and he didn't have any money. It was a long walk home, and he was getting very tired and hungry. He knocked on the door of a cottage to ask for a bite to eat, but the people who lived there hid inside their cottage, and would not answer the door. Thus it went on all day, at all the cottages along the road. The young soldier knocked on every door, but nobody would give him any food.	**Put up SOLDIER to left of COTTAGE.** **Move SOLDIER closer to left of COTTAGE.** **Move SOLDIER to right of COTTAGE. Take down COTTAGE.**
Finally, when he was so hungry that he didn't know how he could go on walking, he knocked at the door of a very nice house. He thought, "Surely these rich people will give me something to eat."	**Put up RICH HOUSE (exterior view) to right and above SOLDIER.**
A woman opened the door just a crack and said, "What do you want?"	**Open door; put up WOMAN behind RICH HOUSE, head showing through doorway.**
The young soldier gave her his best smile and said, "Oh, please, could I have something to eat?"	
The woman said, "No," and started to close the door, but the young soldier asked, "Couldn't I just have a little something to eat?"	**Close door.**
The woman answered, "No! It's been a hard year. We don't have any food. So don't ask again, because we don't have anything to eat."	**Open door.**
But before she could close the door, the young soldier said, "Then I'll just give you something to eat."	**Partly close door.**
The woman asked, "What? I thought you didn't have any food!"	**Open door.**
The soldier answered, "On the road in front of your house I saw a very special stone, a soup stone, I believe it was. Ah, here it is!" And the young man picked up a big smooth stone from the road.	**Put up STONE in SOLDIER's hand.**
The woman asked, "A soup stone, you say? What is that?"	
The soldier answered her, "Why, it's a special stone that will make soup, delicious soup, when it's boiled in a pot of water over a fire. If I had a pot of water, I'd boil you some stone soup right here, right now."	

SCRIPT	FLANNELBOARD
The woman answered, "If all you need is a pot of water, well, I can give you that." So she brought out a big cooking pot and filled it full of water. The young soldier gathered some dry wood and built a fire under the pot. Then he dropped in the big stone, and he watched it boil for a long time.	**Put up POT below RICH HOUSE.** **Put up FIRE under POT. Move STONE to top of POT.**
After awhile the woman asked, "Is the soup ready yet?"	
The soldier answered her, "Just about ready. I can tell by the smell that it's a delicious soup. Of course, it would taste better if I had added salt and pepper. But since I don't have any salt or pepper, we'll just have to eat it plain." And he gave a big sigh.	
But the woman said, "I do have a little salt and pepper." So she brought out the salt and pepper, and added some to the pot of boiling water. Then she asked, "Is the soup ready yet?"	**Put up SALT AND PEPPER in WOMAN's hand.** **Take down SALT AND PEPPER.**
The soldier answered her, "Just about ready. I can tell by the smell that it's a truly delicious soup. Of course, it would taste better if I had added one onion. But since I don't have any onions, we'll just have to eat it plain." And he gave a big sigh.	
But the woman said, "I do have just one little onion left." So she brought out an onion and added it to the pot of boiling water. Then she asked, "Is the soup ready yet?"	**Put up ONION in POT.**
The soldier answered her, "Just about ready. I can tell by the smell that it's an absolutely delicious soup. Of course, it would taste better if I had added some carrots. But since I don't have any carrots, we'll just have to eat it plain." And he gave a big sigh.	
But the woman said, "I might have a few old leftover carrots stored somewhere in the house." So she brought out some carrots and added them to the pot of boiling water. Then she asked, "Is the soup ready yet?"	**Put up CARROTS in POT.**
The soldier answered her, "Just about ready. I can tell by the smell that it's a wonderfully delicious soup. Of course, it would taste better if I had added three potatoes. But since I don't have even one little potato, we'll just have to eat it plain." And he gave a big sigh.	

SCRIPT	FLANNELBOARD

But the woman said, "I think I know where I could get three small potatoes." So she brought out three potatoes and added them to the pot of boiling water. Then she asked, "Is the soup ready yet?"

Put up POTATOES in POT.

The soldier answered her, "Just about ready. I can tell by the smell that it's a marvelously delicious soup. Of course, there is only one thing that could make it better, but that's not important, because I don't have any." The woman looked eagerly at the soldier, but he just sighed and whispered very softly, "Too bad we don't have a few green peas."

Without a word, the woman brought out a handful of green peas from her house and added them to the pot.

Put up PEAS in POT.

After the soup had cooked a little while longer, the soldier said, "Now our good soup is ready." But he did not dish up any soup for them.

Take down FIRE.

Instead, he sighed until the woman asked him, "What's wrong? Didn't you say the soup was good?"

The soldier answered her, "Oh, the *soup* is quite good. I'm just sorry that I can't serve you a real meal, instead of just plain soup. It would taste so good with bread to eat and cider to drink."

The woman opened her door and said, "Since you have furnished such a delicious soup, I will furnish the bread and cider."

Flip over RICH HOUSE. Put up BREAD and JUG on table.

So the woman and the soldier sat down at the table, and they ate all the soup and bread, and they drank all the cider. When they had finished all the food, the woman sighed and said, "Just imagine—a fine, delicious soup from just a *stone*!"

Move WOMAN to right of table, SOLDIER to left of table.

Take down everything out of POT except STONE. Take down BREAD and JUG.

As she said that, the young soldier jumped up from the table and pulled the stone out of the empty soup pot. The woman exclaimed, "Whatever are you doing?"

Move SOLDIER to left of POT. Move STONE to his hand.

He answered, "This stone makes such delicious soup, I must save it to use again tomorrow."

Without another word, he began to walk down the road toward his home. The woman watched until he was almost out of sight. Then she said again, "Just imagine—a fine, delicious soup from just a stone!"

Move SOLDIER to bottom right of board.

Follow-Up Activities

Questions for Discussion or Writing

1. Why did the people in the cottages hide when the young man knocked on their door? Why did the rich woman refuse to give him food?

2. What were the ingredients in the soup? What would you add to make it better? What would you leave out?

Game

Making Soup

Post a large drawing of a soup pot on a wall or bulletin board at the front of the room. Give the children paper, pencils, crayons, and scissors. Have each child draw, color, and cut out a picture of one ingredient of the soup in the story. Attach a loop of masking tape to the back of each paper cutout. Keep a blindfold at the front of the room. Read aloud:

> Each of you will take a turn adding an ingredient to the soup. Hold your paper cutout in your hand. I will blindfold you and turn you around three times. Try to put your cutout in the soup pot. You may feel for the right spot with your hands, but once you stick your cutout to the paper, you may not move it. After everyone has taken a turn, we will see what ingredients will be in our soup today.

Recommended Read-Aloud Books on Related Topics

Versions of This Story

Stone Soup, an Old Tale, told and pictured by Marcia Brown. New York: Scribner, 1947.

Stone Soup, by Ann McGovern. New York: Scholastic, 1968.

Stone Soup, retold by John Warren Stewig. New York: Holiday House, 1991.

Zemach, Harve. *Nail Soup.* Chicago: Follett, 1964.

Stories about Food

Carle, Eric. *The Very Hungry Caterpillar.* New York: Philomel, 1979.

dePaola, Tomie. *Strega Nonna.* Englewood Cliffs, N.J.: Prentice-Hall, 1975.

Priceman, Marjorie. *How to Make an Apple Pie and See the World.* New York: Knopf, 1994.

Soto, Gary. *Too Many Tamales.* New York: Putnam, 1993.

Stories about Unbelievable Happenings

Steig, William. *The Amazing Bone.* New York: Farrar, Straus & Giroux, 1976.

Van Allsburg, Chris. *The Garden of Abdul Gasazi.* Boston: Houghton Mifflin, 1979.

The Three Wishes

Introduction

The origin of this ancient story appears to lie in the legends told in the days before written history. One variant of the tale was recorded in the *Book of Sindibad* (sometimes spelled "Sinbad"), also called *The Book of the Seven Sages,* dating probably from ninth–century Persia. A similar fable appears in the work of the twelfth–century poet Marie de France. Scholars think that her version was really a French translation of an English fable. In 1761 *The Young Misses Magazine* published an English translation of the story originally written in French by Madame Leprince de Beaumont, who had moved to England. The Brothers Grimm collected a similar tale in what is now Germany. Wilhelm Grimm later found parallel stories written in the languages of India, China, and Europe. In the twentieth century Ricardo E. Alegría published a variant of this story in his collection of Puerto Rican folktales.

Despite the tale's wide travels, it remains a simple story for a beginning storyteller to present on the flannelboard. The forest and cottage felt figures fill the board with their colorful scenery. The petty argument of the man and woman characters provides an example of the universality of the human tendency to fight with members of one's own family. Young children may find it comforting to learn that people throughout the world argue over silly disagreements at home, just as their families do.

Set-Up Instructions

Set up the following figures on the flannelboard:

6. Forest, left of center

7. Cottage (interior view), right side

71. Sun, above and to left of cottage

Set up figures on the table, left to right:

19. Man [woodcutter character in this tale]

76. Hatchet

11. Sprite

14. Woman [wife character]

56. Sausage

Read Aloud

<table>
<tr><td align="center">SCRIPT</td><td align="center">FLANNELBOARD</td></tr>
</table>

One morning a woodcutter went into the forest to cut some firewood. He chose a tree and raised his ax to make the first cut. Just then a voice called out, "Stop!"

Put up WOODCUTTER to left of FOREST. Put up HATCHET in WOODCUTTER's hand.

The woodcutter looked all around him, but he did not see anyone nearby. Again he raised his ax, and again the voice called out, "Stop!"

The woodcutter looked all around, but he still did not see anyone nearby. He said, "Where are you? Who are you?"

From inside a tree a wood-sprite appeared and said, "Stop, please stop! Do not cut down this tree."

Put up SPRITE to right of FOREST.

The woodcutter said, "But I have to cut firewood to sell, or my wife and I will have nothing."

The wood-sprite said, "If you will spare these trees, which are my home, then I will give you more than you could ever get from selling firewood. Spare my house, and I will grant you three wishes."

The woodcutter thought for a minute before he said, "I don't need wishes. I need a big stack of firewood to show my wife how hard I worked today. Wishes won't help me."

The wood-sprite answered, "Then I will give your wife the wishes. If you spare my home, the next three wishes made by you or by your wife will be granted."

So the woodcutter agreed, and he walked slowly back home without any firewood.

Take down HATCHET. Move WOODCUTTER to left of COTTAGE.
Put up WIFE to right of fireplace.

When he arrived at the cottage, his wife was cooking. He said, "What's for dinner? I'm really hungry."

His wife said, "Did you get hungry from cutting a lot of firewood this morning?"

He answered, "No, I didn't cut any firewood today. Are there any meat and potatoes?"

She yelled, "No firewood? Then you don't deserve meat and potatoes! You don't even deserve this cabbage soup I'm making."

SCRIPT	FLANNELBOARD
He said sadly, "Just cabbage soup? Oh, I wish I had a big sausage for dinner." Just as the woodcutter spoke, a large sausage appeared on the table.	Put up SAUSAGE on table.
His wife asked, "What is that? Where did it come from?" So her husband told her about the wood-sprite and the three wishes.	
The woodcutter's wife was angry. She yelled, "And you didn't even tell me about the three wishes? You wasted one wish on a sausage without even giving me time to think of a really good wish? You know what you deserve—I wish that sausage would stick to your nose!" Then the woman stopped, and clapped her hands hard over her mouth, because that sausage was stuck hard to her husband's nose.	Move SAUSAGE to WOODCUTTER's nose.
First the woodcutter tried to pull the sausage off while his wife screamed. Then his wife tried to pull it off while he screamed. Finally they had to give it up—wishing had brought that sausage to his nose, and only wishing would take it off.	Move WIFE to right of WOODCUTTER, touching SAUSAGE.
The woodcutter looked at his wife sadly and said, "What are we going to do?"	
She answered, "There's only one thing left to do. The way we have wasted those wishes, we don't deserve to have anything better."	
So together the husband and wife said, "We wish the sausage was gone from this nose." And immediately it was so.	Move SAUSAGE to table.
The man and woman just sat looking at each other for a long time. Finally she said, "Oh, well, we got one good thing out of all this. We actually, finally agreed on *one thing*!"	
"Yes," said her husband, sitting down at the table to eat, "and we got a nice sausage for our dinner, too!"	Move WOODCUTTER down to table, hand touching SAUSAGE.
And I won't tell you what his wife said about that.	

Follow-Up Activities

Questions for Discussion or Writing

1. If you had one wish that would come true, what would it be?

2. With whom do you argue? About what? How do you usually settle your arguments? Name four different ways of settling a dispute, and tell the good points and the bad points of each way.

Game

Wishing Alphabetically

In this game individual children think of something they would like to have that begins with a specific letter of the alphabet. Everyone tries to remember the wishes in alphabetical order. The first child says, "I wish for an _____," filling in the blank with the name of something that begins with the letter *a*. Then the whole group repeats the sentence in unison. Next another student says, "I wish for a _____," filling in the blank with the name of something that begins with *b*. This time the class repeats the sentence but fills in the blank with both the *a* and *b* words: "I wish for an _____ and a _____." Continue wishing until the class has to repeat the sentence with all twenty-six wishes. Keep the pace brisk to increase attention and concentration on the game. Since the repetition is done chorally, the pace can be kept constant even when individuals forget what wish came next. Someone in the group will remember and keep the chorus going.

Recommended Read-Aloud Books on Related Topics

Stories about Wishing

Bond, Felicia. *Poinsettia and Her Family.* New York: Crowell, 1981.

Coombs, Patricia. *The Magic Pot.* New York: Lothrop, Lee & Shepard, 1977.

Oughton, Jerrie. *The Magic Weaver of Rugs: A Tale of the Navajo.* Boston: Houghton Mifflin, 1994.

Steig, William. *Sylvester and the Magic Pebble.* New York: Windmill, 1969.

Williams, Barbara. *Someday, Said Mitchell.* New York: Dutton, 1976.

The Enormous Turnip

Introduction

This folktale is attributed to Russia. It is available in an abundance of versions in English, differing greatly in the numbers and types of animal and human characters that are involved in the story. Two events remain constant in all the versions: one turnip grows much larger than the others, and many characters must work together to pull the turnip from the ground.

Before telling the story, you might want to show the children a real turnip and explain how it grows with the bulb part in the soil and the green leafy part above the ground. Ideally, show the whole turnip, including the leaves, "planted" in a flower-pot of moist soil, so that a child can actually pull the turnip from the soil.

When presenting this story on the flannelboard, encourage the group to name the characters and recite the repeated phrases with you as you read. Point to each character as you say its name to set the pace of the recitation.

Set-Up Instructions

Set up the following figure slightly right of center on the flannelboard:

    5. Garden

Set up figures on the table, left to right:

    20. Man [grandfather character in this tale]

    81. Turnips

    81a. Little Turnip

    82. Big Turnip

    16. Woman [grandmother character]

    14. Woman [mother character]

    19. Man [father character]

    13. Girl

    25. Dog

    26. Cat

    32. Mouse

    33. Beetle

Overlap each felt figure with the previous figure as you place it on the board. Place Grandfather leaning toward the turnip, and everyone else leaning back as though they are pulling hard. Some of their feet will be off the ground.

Read Aloud

——————— SCRIPT ———————

Every day, Grandfather loved to work in his garden. He planted many different vegetables, and he took care of them all. But he took especially good care of the turnips. As the turnips grew, he picked them, and he cooked them and ate them for dinner. Except for one turnip.

Grandfather left one turnip in the ground all summer. He watered the turnip, and he pulled all the weeds around the turnip, and he took especially good care of that one turnip. Until at last it grew into a big, giant, spectacular, *enormous* turnip!

Finally Grandfather decided to pull up that enormous turnip. He grabbed the top of the turnip, and he pulled. He heaved, he strained, and he pulled, but the turnip stayed in the ground.

Grandmother came out to help Grandfather. Grandmother grabbed onto Grandfather, and Grandfather grabbed the turnip, and they pulled. They heaved, they strained, and they pulled, but the turnip stayed in the ground.

Then Mother came out to help. Mother grabbed Grandmother, Grandmother grabbed Grandfather, and Grandfather grabbed the turnip, and they pulled. They heaved, they strained, and they pulled, but the turnip stayed in the ground.

Then Father came out to help. Father grabbed Mother, Mother grabbed Grandmother, Grandmother grabbed Grandfather, and Grandfather grabbed the turnip, and they pulled. They heaved, they strained, and they pulled, but the turnip stayed in the ground.

Then the little girl came out to help. The little girl grabbed Father, Father grabbed Mother, Mother grabbed Grandmother, Grandmother grabbed Grandfather, and Grandfather grabbed the turnip, and they pulled. They heaved, they strained, and they pulled, but the turnip stayed in the ground.

— FLANNELBOARD —

Put up GRANDFATHER to left of GARDEN.

Put up TURNIPS in middle of GARDEN.

Take down TURNIPS; put up LITTLE TURNIP.

Take down LITTLE TURNIP; put up BIG TURNIP.

Move GRANDFATHER to BIG TURNIP.

Put up GRANDMOTHER to left of GRANDFATHER.

Put up MOTHER to left of GRANDMOTHER.

Put up FATHER to left of MOTHER.

Put up GIRL to left of FATHER.

SCRIPT	FLANNELBOARD
Then the dog came out to help. The dog grabbed the little girl, the little girl grabbed Father, Father grabbed Mother, Mother grabbed Grandmother, Grandmother grabbed Grandfather, and Grandfather grabbed the turnip, and they pulled. They heaved, they strained, and they pulled, but the turnip stayed in the ground.	**Put up DOG to left of GIRL.**
Grandfather said, "We need a lot more help."	
Then the cat came out to help. The cat grabbed the dog, the dog grabbed the little girl, the little girl grabbed Father, Father grabbed Mother, Mother grabbed Grandmother, Grandmother grabbed Grandfather, and Grandfather grabbed the turnip, and they pulled. They heaved, they strained, and they pulled, but the turnip stayed in the ground.	**Put up CAT to left of DOG.**
Grandfather said, "We need a little more help."	
Then the mouse came out to help. The mouse grabbed the cat, the cat grabbed the dog, the dog grabbed the little girl, the little girl grabbed Father, Father grabbed Mother, Mother grabbed Grandmother, Grandmother grabbed Grandfather, and Grandfather grabbed the turnip, and they pulled. They heaved, they strained, and they pulled, but the turnip stayed in the ground.	**Put up MOUSE to left of CAT, tails together.**
Grandfather said, "We need a tiny bit more help."	
They all stood there and waited awhile. Slowly, a tiny little beetle walked up to the long line. The beetle grabbed the mouse, the mouse grabbed the cat, the cat grabbed the dog, the dog grabbed the little girl, the little girl grabbed Father, Father grabbed Mother, Mother grabbed Grandmother, Grandmother grabbed Grandfather, and Grandfather grabbed the turnip, and they pulled. They heaved, they strained, and they pulled, and the turnip popped out of the ground. The turnip fell on top of Grandfather, Grandfather fell on top of Grandmother, Grandmother fell on Mother, Mother fell on Father, Father fell on the little girl, the little girl fell on the dog, the dog fell on the cat, and the cat fell on the mouse. Fortunately, the beetle ran away before anybody could fall on him. Then, they were all so hungry from so much hard work that they ate up the whole enormous turnip for dinner.	**Put up BEETLE to left of MOUSE.** **Move BIG TURNIP to left, then to GRANDFATHER's head. Move GRANDFATHER to left. Move GRANDMOTHER to left, then move MOTHER, FATHER, GIRL, DOG, and CAT to left. Move BEETLE to left side of board.** **Take down BIG TURNIP.**

Follow-Up Activities

Questions for Discussion or Writing

1. Who pulled the turnip from the ground? What would have happened if one of the characters had let go before the turnip came out? How would you have pulled the turnip? Think of several different ways to do this.

2. Turnips grow in the ground. Where do other vegetables grow? Read about peanuts, carrots, beans, corn, or lettuce in a book or encyclopedia. What part of each plant do people eat? Name some foods that people eat that are seeds, leaves, flowers, fruits, and roots.

Activities

Science Teamwork

1. Find a piece of furniture that is moveable but too heavy for a person to move easily. Choose something that is low to the ground so that it will not topple over, such as a desk or table. Try these ways to move it a couple of feet along the floor. First, one person pushes. Then try two people pushing from the same side. (This is not a contest to see who can push hardest.) Try to move the piece of furniture with two people on each end, lifting and pushing toward the side (not two pushing forward and two pulling backward). Think about why you should not have two of the people pulling the heavy furniture toward them; what would happen when the furniture moved?

2. Try lifting one book, then two, then a whole stack. Books are surprisingly heavy. Fill a bag with several books, too heavy for one person to lift and carry. To demonstrate how a team can lift the books easily, set the bag on a blanket or large towel. Position several people around the edges of the blanket or towel, with each person squatting with bent knees and holding the blanket or towel with both hands. On the count of three, the people stand up. Ask them if the books seemed very heavy to lift. (This activity is also a demonstration of the proper way to lift safely with the legs rather than with the back; be sure the lifters do the job by standing from a squatting position, not by bending over with straight legs.)

Recommended Read-Aloud Books on Related Topics

Other Version of "The Enormous Turnip"

Lottridge, Celia B. *Ten Small Tales*. New York: Margaret K. McElderry, 1994.

Stories about Things That Grow

Asch, Frank. *Popcorn: A Frank Asch Bear Story*. New York: Parent's, 1979.

Hutchins, Pat. *Titch*. New York: Macmillan, 1971.

Kent, Jack. *The Caterpillar and the Polliwog*. Englewood Cliffs, N.J.: Prentice-Hall, 1982.

McPhail, David. *Pig Pig Grows Up*. New York: Dutton, 1980.

Introduction

Although this tale appeared in the collections of folktales published by Perrault and by the Brothers Grimm, it is not included in very many modern collections or children's picture books. Yet, the story is moderately easy for a storyteller to present on the flannelboard, and it has considerable visual appeal because of the brightly colored frog and diamond-cluster felt figures used with detailed scenery in the forest, water, cottage interior, and distant castle pieces.

"Diamonds and Toads" provides the satisfaction of virtue rewarded and evil punished in a most unusual way. Older children delight in the grotesque aspect of awful things coming out of people's mouths.

Set-Up Instructions

Set up the following figures on the flannelboard:

7. Cottage (interior view), near left bottom edge

6. Forest, to the right of the cottage and several inches above bottom edge

8. Water [pond in this tale], at right bottom edge

Set up figures on the table, left to right:

17. Woman [mother character in this tale]

15. Woman [rude daughter character]

14. Woman [kind daughter character]

78. Jug

16. Woman [old woman character]

11. Fairy

63. Diamonds

28. Frog [toad character]

18, 18a. Man [prince character] with Crown

2. Distant Castle

Read Aloud

<table>
<tr><td colspan="1">——— SCRIPT ———</td><td>— FLANNELBOARD —</td></tr>
</table>

SCRIPT	FLANNELBOARD
Once upon a time, in a cottage on the edge of a forest, there lived a woman who had two daughters. One daughter was as haughty and mean as her mother. The two of them complained and griped and insulted and said rude things all day long, every day, day in and day out. Never a kind word came from their lips, and never a kind deed came from their hands.	**Put up MOTHER to left of chair.** **Put up RUDE DAUGHTER to right of MOTHER.**
But the other daughter was just as kind and sweet and good as her sister was mean and selfish and rude. Every day, while the mother and the mean sister argued about whose turn it was to walk through the woods to the pond to get water for washing and drinking, the gentle sister would take the water jug and walk through the woods to fill up the jug at the pond.	**Put up KIND DAUGHTER to right of RUDE DAUGHTER.** **Put up JUG in KIND DAUGHTER's hand. Move KIND DAUGHTER and JUG to just above POND.**
One day, after the gentle sister had filled up the heavy water jug and was starting to walk back home with it, she saw an old woman in the woods right beside her. The old woman said, "Please, may I have a drink of water from your jug? I am terribly hot and thirsty."	**Put up OLD WOMAN to left of KIND DAUGHTER.**
The kind sister tilted the jug over so that the old woman could get a drink. She did not hesitate to help the old woman, even though it meant that she would have to go back to the pond to wash the jug and refill it before she could start back home.	**Move top of JUG toward OLD WOMAN.**
Suddenly, the old woman disappeared, and in her place appeared a beautiful fairy, who flew up into the air and touched the girl's head with her wand. The fairy said, "In return for your kindness, I grant that forevermore, when you speak, a wonderful present will come from your mouth."	**Take down OLD WOMAN. Put up FAIRY to right above KIND DAUGHTER.**
Wondering greatly at the meaning of the fairy's words, the gentle sister refilled the jug and walked back home. When she arrived there, her mother and sister began to yell at her for being late with the water.	**Move KIND DAUGHTER and JUG to right of RUDE DAUGHTER.**
The kind daughter said, "I'm sorry," and a cluster of diamonds came out of her mouth.	**Put up DIAMONDS to left of KIND DAUGHTER's mouth, partly hidden behind her head.**
Mother cried, "Look look! What is this? Where did these come from?"	
As the girl explained what had happened in the woods, even more diamonds came out of her mouth.	**Move DIAMONDS to left so they all show.**

SCRIPT	FLANNELBOARD

SCRIPT

FLANNELBOARD

Her mother grabbed the diamonds and said to her other daughter, "Right now, daughter, you go give the fairy a drink of water, too! If your stupid sister can get diamonds, just think what things you can get, even better than jewels! Go on, right now!"

Move DIAMONDS to MOTHER's hand.

Move JUG to RUDE DAUGHTER's hand.

The mean sister argued and stamped her foot, but finally she took the jug and stomped off through the forest. She stopped when she saw the fairy flying over her head. The rude daughter called, "Hey, you up there! Come down here right now."

Move RUDE DAUGHTER and JUG to below FAIRY.

The fairy answered, "Do you have a present for me?"

The mean sister answered, "No, but I'm going to crack you on the head with this jug if you don't give *me* a present!"

The fairy frowned and answered, "A present you will have, in return for your own behavior. Every time you speak, something very surprising will come out of your mouth."

Take down FAIRY.

Then the rude sister threw down the water jug, and she ran back home to tell her mother what the fairy had said. The girl opened her mouth to say, "Mother," and a big green toad came hopping out of her throat. She screamed, and the toad hopped off her tongue. She clamped her mouth shut and refused to say another word for fear another toad would come hopping out of her mouth.

Take down JUG. Move RUDE DAUGHTER to right of MOTHER.

Put up TOAD on RUDE DAUGHTER's mouth.

Move TOAD down.

Her mother yelled so angrily and so loud and long that both sisters ran out into the woods. The mean sister wandered by herself in the woods with nobody to keep her company except the toads that came out of her mouth every time she spoke. But the sweet and kind sister had not gone very far when she met a young prince out walking in the woods. "Good day," he said.

Move RUDE DAUGHTER to left side of FOREST, and KIND DAUGHTER to right side.

Move TOAD to RUDE DAUGHTER's mouth.

Put up PRINCE to left of KIND DAUGHTER.

She answered, "Good day, kind sir," and a cluster of diamonds plopped out of her mouth and onto the Prince.

Move DIAMONDS to left of KIND DAUGHTER's mouth.

After she had explained what was happening, causing the Prince's hands to fill up completely with diamonds, he asked her to come to the castle with him to be his wife. Together they walked toward the castle that was to be their home as they lived happily ever after.

Move DIAMONDS to PRINCE's hands.

Put up DISTANT CASTLE at top right.

Follow-Up Activities

Questions for Discussion or Writing

1. If diamonds came out of your mouth whenever you talked, how would it change your life? What would happen when you sang or whistled, or when you played with your friends? What would you do with the diamonds? How would you explain to people what was happening?

2. If toads came out of your mouth whenever you talked, what would you do with the toads? How would you explain to people what was happening?

Game

Diamonds and Toads

Everyone sits in a large circle, facing the center, except for one person who will be It. It walks around the outside of the circle, touching each child on the head and saying "diamond." After touching several heads and calling each one "diamond," It will touch someone's head and say "toad." It runs around the outside of the circle chased by the child who was picked. The first one to arrive back in the chosen child's spot in the circle stays there, and the other child is It for the next round.

Recommended Read-Aloud Books on Related Topics

Story Similar to "Diamonds and Toads"

Steptoe, John. *Mufaro's Beautiful Daughters: An African Tale.* New York: Lothrop, Lee & Shepard, 1987.

Stories about Words and Names

dePaola, Tomie. *Oliver Button Is a Sissy.* New York: Harcourt, 1979.

Lester, Helen. *A Porcupine Named Fluffy.* Boston: Houghton Mifflin, 1972.

Van Allsburg, Chris. *Jumanji.* Boston: Houghton Mifflin, 1981.

Waber, Ira. *Ira Sleeps Over.* Boston: Houghton Mifflin, 1972.

Yolen, Jane. *Sleeping Ugly.* New York: Coward, McCann & Geoghegan, 1981.

The Gingerbread Man

Introduction

"The Gingerbread Man" is the same basic story told in Norway as "The Pancake," in England as "The Journey Cake," in Scotland as "The Wee Bannock," and in the United States as the traditional tale of the gingerbread boy. "The Gingerbread Man" is a storytime favorite for preschool children, who can be heard chanting the refrain in their games of tag: "Run, run, as fast as you can. You can't catch me; I'm the Gingerbread Man." This is a cumulative tale, with one character at a time added throughout the story. Therefore, the story of the gingerbread cookie that comes to life and eludes all pursuers except for one is well-suited to presentation on a flannelboard. The large flannelboard recommended in this book offers enough room for all the characters to be shown as they join in the chase.

Set-Up Instructions

Set up the following figures on the flannelboard:

7. Cottage (interior view), eight inches from the left edge

71. Sun, in upper-right corner

Set up figures on the table, left to right:

16. Woman [old woman character in this tale]

20. Man [old man character]

21. Gingerbread Man [cookie]

14. Woman [farm woman character]

31. Donkey

25. Dog

34. Fox

8. Water [stream]

Read Aloud

<table>
<tr><th>SCRIPT</th><th>FLANNELBOARD</th></tr>
<tr><td>

Once upon a time there lived a little old woman and a little old man. They lived all alone in their little old house, and they were lonely for a little young child. So one day the little old woman made a large gingerbread cookie in the shape of a little man. She cut the gingerbread dough in the shape of arms, legs, and a head. Then she made his eyes and nose and mouth out of raisins and nuts, and she put the cookie into the fire to bake.

</td><td>

Put up OLD WOMAN to left of table. Put up OLD MAN to left of OLD WOMAN.

Put up COOKIE on table.

</td></tr>
<tr><td>

After awhile the little old woman checked to see if the cookie was done. Much to her surprise, the little gingerbread man jumped out of the fire and began to run around the room on his little short legs.

</td><td>

Move COOKIE to fireplace. Move OLD WOMAN to left of fire.

Move COOKIE to basket, then to bed, then to right of fire.

</td></tr>
<tr><td>

The little old woman chased the gingerbread man around and around the room, calling out, "Stop! Stop!" But the gingerbread man kept on running.

</td><td></td></tr>
<tr><td>

As he ran he said, "Run, run, as fast as you can! You can't catch me; I'm the gingerbread man!" Finally, he ran out the door of the little old house, and he started running down the road. The little old woman ran out after him, but the gingerbread man outran her.

</td><td>

Move COOKIE to middle of board.

Move OLD WOMAN to left of COOKIE.

</td></tr>
<tr><td>

Outside in the fields, the gingerbread man ran even faster. When the little old man saw what had happened, he chased after the gingerbread man to try to catch him. But the gingerbread man just looked back over his shoulder, and laughed, and said, "Run, run, as fast as you can! You can't catch me; I'm the gingerbread man! I've run away from a little old woman, and I can run away from you, I can, I can." The little old man ran after him, but the gingerbread man outran him.

</td><td>

Move COOKIE to right. Take down COTTAGE. Move OLD MAN to left of COOKIE.

</td></tr>
<tr><td>

When a farm woman who was working in the fields saw what had happened, she left the fields and began to chase after the gingerbread man. But the gingerbread man just looked back over his shoulder, and laughed, and said, "Run, run, as fast as you can! You can't catch me; I'm the gingerbread man! I've run away from a little old woman and a little old man, and I can run away from you, I can, I can." The farm woman ran after him, but the gingerbread man outran her.

</td><td>

Move COOKIE to right.

Put up FARM WOMAN at middle left. Move FARM WOMAN to left of COOKIE.

Move COOKIE to right.

</td></tr>
</table>

The Gingerbread Man **99**

SCRIPT	FLANNELBOARD
When the donkey who was grazing in the pasture saw what had happened, he left the pasture and began to chase after the gingerbread man. But the gingerbread man just looked back over his shoulder, and laughed, and said, "Run, run, as fast as you can! You can't catch me; I'm the gingerbread man! I've run away from a little old woman and a little old man, and a farmer, and I can run away from you, I can, I can." The donkey ran after him, but the gingerbread man outran him.	**Put up DONKEY at middle left. Move DONKEY to left of COOKIE.**
	Move COOKIE to right.
When a dog who was playing in the sunshine saw what had happened, he began to chase the gingerbread man. But the gingerbread man just looked back over his shoulder, and laughed, and said, "Run, run, as fast as you can! You can't catch me; I'm the gingerbread man! I've run away from a little old woman and a little old man, and a farmer, and a donkey, and I can run away from you, I can, I can." The dog ran after him, but the gingerbread man outran him.	**Put up DOG at middle left. Move DOG to left of COOKIE.**
	Move COOKIE to right.
When a fox who was sunning himself near the stream saw what had happened, he jumped up, and he began to chase the gingerbread man. But the gingerbread man just looked back over his shoulder, and laughed, and said, "Run, run, as fast as you can! You can't catch me; I'm the gingerbread man! I've run away from a little old woman and a little old man, and a farmer, and a donkey, and a dog, and I can run away from you, I can, I can." The fox ran after him, but the gingerbread man outran him.	**Put up FOX at bottom left. Move FOX to left of COOKIE.**
	Move COOKIE to right.
Soon the gingerbread man came to a stream. He could not swim, and he was afraid that the animals and people chasing him would eat him up. He didn't know what to do. The fox was the first to reach him. The gingerbread man said, "Oh, please, Mr. Fox, don't eat me!"	**Put up STREAM below COOKIE.** **Move FOX very close to COOKIE.**
The fox looked back over his shoulder at all the others who would like to share the cookie with him, and he said, "Oh, no, gingerbread man, I don't want to eat you!"	
The gingerbread man asked doubtfully, "You don't?"	
"No," answered the fox, "I am trying to save you from all those others who want to eat you! Right now, for example, I'll help you get away from them. Just jump onto my tail, and I'll take you across to the other side of the stream."	

So the gingerbread man jumped onto the fox's tail, and the fox started to swim across the stream. Soon he said, "Oh, gingerbread man, the water is getting deeper. You'd better move up to a higher place on my back." So the gingerbread man moved onto the fox's back, and the fox swam on.	**Move COOKIE to tail of FOX. Move FOX to edge of STREAM.** **Move COOKIE to back of FOX. Move FOX to middle of STREAM.**
Soon the fox called out again, "Oh, gingerbread man, the water is getting much deeper. You'd better move to a higher place on my shoulder." So the gingerbread man moved onto the fox's shoulder, and the fox swam on.	**Move COOKIE to shoulder of FOX.**
In a few minutes the fox said, "This is the deepest part of the stream, gingerbread man. Soon all of me will be under the water except my nose. You'd better move on up now." So the gingerbread man moved onto the fox's nose, and the fox swam on. But as the fox swam, he opened his mouth, and the gingerbread man began to slide right in, and the fox ate him all up.	**Move FOX further right in STREAM.** **Move COOKIE to nose of FOX. Move FOX to right in STREAM. Take down COOKIE.**
By the time the fox reached the other side of the stream, all the animals and people who had been chasing the gingerbread man were looking to see where the cookie could have disappeared. But all they saw was the fox asleep on dry land on the other side of the stream.	**Move FOX to right corner below STREAM, on his back.**

Follow-Up Activities

Questions for Discussion or Writing

1. Why did the woman in the story make the gingerbread cookie in the shape of a person? When she saw him come to life, how do you think she felt? When she saw him disappear, how do you think she felt? What do you think she did after that?

2. When the gingerbread man came out of the oven, he saw the world for the first time. What did he see as he looked around the house? What did he see as he ran along the road? What did he hear, feel, and smell for the first time that day?

Game

Gingerbread Man Capture

This game is played like London Bridge. Two children stand facing each other with their clasped hands raised to make a bridge. Everyone else forms a single line that runs under the bridge. The two bridge holders chant, "Run, run, as fast as you can. You can't catch me; I'm the gingerbread man." On the word *man,* the bridge holders bring down their hands to capture the child who is directly under their hands at that time. The captured child replaces one of the bridge holders, and the game begins again.

Recommended Read-Aloud Books on Related Topics

Stories about Going to New Places and Learning New Things

Gackenbach, Dick. *Claude and Pepper.* New York: Seabury, 1977.

Hutchins, Pat. *The Tale of Thomas Mead.* New York: Greenwillow, 1980.

Kent, Jack. *Joey Runs Away.* Englewood Cliffs, N.J.: Prentice-Hall, 1985.

Pinkwater, Daniel. *Guys from Space.* New York: Macmillan, 1989.

Say, Allen. *Grandfather's Journey.* Boston: Houghton Mifflin, 1993.

Sendak, Maurice. *Where the Wild Things Are.* New York: Harper & Row, 1963.

Taylor, C. J. *The Ghost and Lone Warrior: An Arapaho Legend.* Montreal: Tundra, 1991.

Tombert, Ann. *Little Fox Goes to the End of the World.* New York: Crown, 1976.

The Old Woman and her Pig

Introduction

"The Old Woman and Her Pig" is usually assumed to be of English origin because the coin is referred to as a sixpence in so many versions. It is a cumulative nursery story similar to "The House That Jack Built" and "The Old Woman Who Swallowed a Fly."

Before presenting this tale, show the stile felt figure on the flannelboard and explain its function: To cross a fence without opening the gate and perhaps letting out the livestock behind the fence, a person can go up these steps called a "stile" and down the steps on the other side of the fence. Livestock will not ordinarily go over the stile.

Set-Up Instructions

Set up the following figure on the flannelboard in the upper right corner:

> 7. Cottage (exterior view)

Set up figures on the table, left to right:

> 16. Woman [old woman character in this tale]
>
> 79. Coin
>
> 45. Stile
>
> 37. Pig
>
> 25. Dog
>
> 50. Stick
>
> 51. Fire
>
> 8. Water [pond]
>
> 36. Ox
>
> 19. Man [butcher character]
>
> 65. Rope (coiled loosely)
>
> 32. Mouse
>
> 26. Cat
>
> 27. Cow
>
> 52. Hay
>
> 54. Pail

Read Aloud

SCRIPT	FLANNELBOARD

Long ago, in a cottage far away, there lived an old woman. One day she found a huge gold coin in her garden. She picked it up, and she thought of all the things she could buy with it. Finally the woman decided to walk into town to the market. To get to market she had to cross a tall stone fence, so she walked up one side of the stile, over the top, and down the other side, and into town to the market. There she bought a pig and started to walk home. But the pig would not go over the stile.

Put up OLD WOMAN to left of COTTAGE. Put up COIN in OLD WOMAN's hand.

Put up STILE to left above OLD WOMAN.

Move OLD WOMAN to far left; take down COIN. Put up PIG to right of OLD WOMAN.

The old woman said, "Pig, pig, go over the stile, or I shan't get home tonight." But the pig would not go over the stile.

Along came a dog. The old woman said, "Dog, dog, bite pig because pig won't go over the stile, and I shan't get home tonight." But the dog would not.

Put up DOG under OLD WOMAN.

Then the old woman saw a stick on the ground. She said, "Stick, stick, hit dog because dog won't bite pig, so pig won't go over the stile, and I shan't get home tonight." But the stick would not.

Put up STICK to right of DOG.

Then the old woman saw a little fire smoldering in the brush nearby. She said, "Fire, fire, burn stick because stick won't hit dog, so dog won't bite pig, so pig won't go over the stile, and I shan't get home tonight." But the fire would not.

Put up FIRE to right of STICK.

Then the old woman saw a pond full of water. She said, "Water, water, quench fire because fire won't burn stick, so stick won't hit dog, so dog won't bite pig, so pig won't go over the stile, and I shan't get home tonight." But the water would not.

Put up POND to right of FIRE.

Then the old woman saw an ox walking toward its home after working all day. She said, "Ox, ox, drink water because water won't quench fire, so fire won't burn stick, so stick won't hit dog, so dog won't bite pig, so pig won't go over the stile, and I shan't get home tonight." But the ox would not.

Put up OX to right of POND.

Then along the road came a man. The old woman recognized him; he was the butcher who ran the meat market. She said, "Butcher, butcher, kill ox because ox won't drink water, so water won't quench fire, so fire won't burn stick, so stick won't hit dog, so dog won't bite pig, so pig won't go over the stile, and I shan't get home tonight." But the man would not.

Put up BUTCHER above OX.

Then the old woman saw a piece of rope. She said, "Rope, rope, hang butcher because butcher won't kill ox, so ox won't drink water, so water won't quench fire, so fire won't burn stick, so stick won't hit dog, so dog won't bite pig, so pig won't go over the stile, and I shan't get home tonight." But the rope would not.

Put up ROPE to left above BUTCHER.

Then the old woman saw a little mouse nibbling some plants at the side of the road. She said, "Mouse, mouse, gnaw rope because rope won't hang butcher, so butcher won't kill ox, so ox won't drink water, so water won't quench fire, so fire won't burn stick, so stick won't hit dog, so dog won't bite pig, so pig won't go over the stile, and I shan't get home tonight." But the mouse would not.

Put up MOUSE to left above ROPE.

Along the road came a cat. The old woman said, "Cat, cat, attack mouse because mouse won't gnaw rope, so rope won't hang butcher, so butcher won't kill ox, so ox won't drink water, so water won't quench fire, so fire won't burn stick, so stick won't hit dog, so dog won't bite pig, so pig won't go over the stile, and I shan't get home tonight." But the cat would not.

Put up CAT to left of MOUSE.

The old woman thought about all the things she wanted to happen to everyone around her. They were all bad things to happen. She thought that perhaps if she asked for something good to happen she would get what she wanted. So when she saw a cow coming along the road, she said, "Cow, cow, give milk to the cat."

Put up COW to left of CAT.

The cow answered her, "If you will get me some nice hay to eat I will give the cat some nice milk to drink."

So the old woman looked around, and she found some hay and brought it to the cow. As soon as the cow started eating the hay, she gave the old woman a whole pail of milk. So the old woman gave the cat the pail of milk. Then the cat started to attack the mouse, and the mouse started to gnaw the rope, and the rope started to hang the butcher, and the butcher started to kill the ox, and the ox started to drink the water, and the water started to quench the fire, and the fire started to burn the stick, and the stick started to hit the dog, and the dog started to bite the pig. The pig became so scared that he ran and jumped right over the stile without even stopping. So the old woman went over the stile, saying to herself, "I *shall* get home tonight." And she did.

Put up HAY to left below COW.

Put up PAIL to left of CAT.
Take down CAT, then MOUSE,
  then ROPE,
  then BUTCHER, then OX,
  then POND, then FIRE,
  then STICK,
  then DOG.
Move PIG to right of STILE.
Move OLD WOMAN to top of STILE.

Follow-Up Activities

Questions for Discussion or Writing

1. How would you have persuaded the pig to go over the stile? What would you have done first, next, and last? Why would your method have worked?

2. Did people ever persuade you to do something that you did not want to do? How did they persuade you? What did you do? Were you glad or sorry that you did it?

Activity

Sequencing the Story

Put all the felt figures from this story (except the coin) on the flannelboard in mixed-up order. Read the following aloud.

> Most of the action in this story took place at the very end. Let's try to remember the order of all the events that happened. Each time we remember together what happened next, I'll put up the felt figure to illustrate that action, and we'll recite the action together. We'll start with "*Woman, woman, give hay to the cow.*" I'll put up the felt figure for the woman, then the hay, then the cow. What happened next?

Pause before picking up the next felt figure to give students time to recall what happened next. Then recite in unison as you put up the next felt figures in line:

> Cow, cow, give milk to the cat;
> cat, cat, attack the mouse, etc.

Recommended Read-Aloud Books on Related Topics

Stories about Pigs

Heine, Helme. *The Pigs' Wedding.* New York: Atheneum, 1979.

Lobel, Arnold. *The Book of Pigericks.* New York: Harper & Row, 1983.

McPhail, David. *Pig Pig and the Magic Photo Album.* New York: Dutton, 1986.

Stories about Making Things Happen

Gershator, Phillis. *The Iroko-Man: A Yoruba Folktale.* New York: Orchard, 1994.

Van Allsburg, Chris. *The Garden of Abdul Gasazi.* Boston: Houghton Mifflin, 1979.

Lazy Jack

Introduction

A young man named Jack is the principal character in many folktales collected in Britain as well as in southern Appalachia among people of British ancestry. The name *Jack* is a very common British name; like the familiar figure "Hans" used in many German folktales, "Jack" may serve as a sort of generic male character with few distinguishing characteristics. Like most fairy tale characters, Jack is never described beyond a single word such as *lazy* or *brave*.

There is a whole cycle of stories about Jack. Before presenting "Lazy Jack," ask children if they have ever heard a story about a boy named Jack. (They may mention "Jack and the Beanstalk" or "Jack the Giant Killer.") Also ask if they have ever heard a story called "Clever Hans," which is very similar to the story "Lazy Jack."

Set-Up Instructions

Set up the flannelboard vertically for this story, and set up the following figure on it:

    1. Castle

Set up figures on the table, left to right:

    15, 15b. Woman [princess character in this tale] with Crown

    20, 20a. Man [king character] with Crown

    8. Water [stream]

    7. Cottage (interior view)

    19. Man [Jack character]

    16. Woman [mother character]

    79. Coin

    27. Cow

    78. Jug

    26. Cat

    46a. Bread with String

    31. Donkey

Read Aloud

<table>
<tr><th style="text-align:center">SCRIPT</th><th style="text-align:center">FLANNELBOARD</th></tr>
<tr><td>

Long ago in a lovely castle a beautiful princess lived with her father. When they walked around the castle they saw many delightful things, but these things did not make the princess happy. She never smiled, never talked, and never laughed.

</td><td>

Put up PRINCESS to left of CASTLE, KING to right of PRINCESS.

</td></tr>
<tr><td>

Because the heart of the princess was sad, her father's heart was sad also. He often said, "Oh, if only she could learn to laugh!"

</td><td>

Take down PRINCESS, KING, and CASTLE.

</td></tr>
<tr><td>

A distance away from the castle, there was a stream full of fast-running water. On the other side of the stream, in a small cottage, there lived a big, lazy boy, called Lazy Jack, and his mother. Every day while his mother worked in the house and on the farm, Lazy Jack slept and rested and watched his mother work.

</td><td>

Put up STREAM in center.

Put up COTTAGE at bottom right.

Put up JACK lying on bed. Put up MOTHER to left of bed.

</td></tr>
<tr><td>

Early on a Monday morning, Jack's mother decided that something had to change. So she said to him, "Jack, don't be so lazy. You get up, and go out to work. And don't come home until your day's work is done and you have your pay in your hand."

</td><td>

Move JACK to upright position.

</td></tr>
<tr><td>

Jack said, "My pay in my hand. I'll remember." And he walked down the road, across the stream, and over to the nearest farm, where he found work. All day long he worked.

</td><td>

Move JACK to top right.

</td></tr>
<tr><td>

At the end of the day the farmer told Jack, "Tomorrow you will learn to milk the cows." The farmer gave Jack a gold coin as his first day's pay, and Jack started walking toward home.

</td><td>

Put up COIN on JACK's hand.

</td></tr>
<tr><td>

When Jack jumped over the stream, the gold coin fell out of his hand and into the stream. Jack walked home with no pay.

</td><td>

Move JACK to top of STREAM. Take down COIN.

</td></tr>
<tr><td>

When he reached home, Jack told his mother how he had lost the coin. She yelled, "That was foolish, Jack! You should have carried your pay in your pocket."

</td><td>

Move JACK to right of MOTHER.

</td></tr>
<tr><td>

Jack repeated, "In my pocket. I'll remember, and I'll do it next time."

</td><td></td></tr>
<tr><td>

On Tuesday, Jack returned to the farm. He worked all day taking care of the cows and milking them.

</td><td>

Move JACK to top center. Put up COW to right of JACK.

</td></tr>
<tr><td>

At the end of the day, the farmer said to Jack, "Tomorrow you will learn to make cheese from the extra milk." He gave Jack a jug of milk for his second day's pay.

</td><td>

Put up JUG on JACK's hand.

</td></tr>
<tr><td>

Jack poured the milk into his pocket, and he walked home.

</td><td>

Take down JUG.

</td></tr>
</table>

SCRIPT	FLANNELBOARD

When he reached his house, he told his mother what he had done. His mother said, "That was foolish, Jack. Next time, you should carry your pay on top of your head and hold it with both hands."

Move JACK to right of MOTHER.

Jack repeated, "On top of my head, with both hands. I'll remember, and I'll do it next time."

On Wednesday, Jack returned to the farm. He worked all day, learning to make cheese out of the milk.

Move JACK to left of COW.

At the end of the day the farmer said to Jack, "Tomorrow you will learn to bake bread." He gave Jack a cat for his third day's pay.

Jack held the cat on top of his head with both hands, and began to walk toward home.

Put up CAT on JACK's head.

When he reached his house, he had scratches all over his head, and hands, and arms. His mother set the cat on the ground. She said, "That was foolish, Jack. Next time, you should tie a long string around your pay and hold the string and let it walk home beside you."

Move JACK to right of MOTHER. Move CAT to right of JACK.

Jack repeated, "Tie a string, and let it walk beside me. I'll remember, and I'll do it next time."

On Thursday Jack learned to bake bread. All day he worked hard.

Move JACK to left of COW. Take down COW.

At the end of the day the farmer said, "Tomorrow you will take care of the donkeys in the stable." He gave Jack a big loaf of bread for his fourth day's pay.

Jack was prepared this time. He took a long string from his pocket, and he tied it around the bread. Then he set the bread on the ground and he started to walk home. He walked down the road, across the stream, and all the way home.

Put up BREAD WITH STRING in JACK's hand.

Move JACK and BREAD WITH STRING to top of STREAM.

When he got home, his mother took one look at the wet, muddy bread tied to the end of the string. Even the cat would not eat it. His mother yelled, "Jack, that was so foolish! Next time, carry your pay on your shoulder."

Move JACK and BREAD WITH STRING to right of MOTHER.

Jack repeated, "Oh my shoulder. I'll remember, and I'll do it next time."

SCRIPT	FLANNELBOARD
On Friday Jack walked again down the road and over the stream to the farm. All day long he cared for the donkeys, feeding and watering and washing and brushing them.	Move JACK to top center. Put up DONKEY to right of JACK.
At the end of the day the farmer said, "Tomorrow is Saturday, so you won't have to come to work." He gave Jack a donkey for his fifth day's pay.	
Jack worked very hard to lift the heavy donkey to his shoulder. The donkey's feet fit on his shoulders, but the rest of it stuck up over Jack's head. Jack started walking toward home.	Move DONKEY to JACK's back.
It was much too hard to walk across the stream with the donkey on his shoulder, so Jack walked down a different road. He walked right by the castle. The donkey was balanced with its hooves on Jack's shoulders and its body on Jack's head, just as they passed in front of the castle.	Take down STREAM, COTTAGE, MOTHER, BREAD WITH STRING, and CAT. Put up CASTLE. Move JACK and DONKEY to bottom right.
At that exact time the princess and her father were taking their daily walk around the castle. When the princess saw Jack staggering by with a donkey balanced on top of his shoulders, she stared. Then she opened her mouth, and she took a breath, and she laughed. She looked at Jack, and she laughed until she lay right down on the ground and kept right on laughing.	Put up PRINCESS and KING to left of JACK. Move PRINCESS to lie on her back.
When the princess's father yelled for Jack to stop, Jack was frightened. He thought the king was angry with him. But the princess and her father were so happy and grateful to Jack for getting the princess to laugh that they asked Jack to come live at the castle with them. Jack married the beautiful princess, and for the rest of their lives the princess, her father, Jack, his mother, and the donkey all lived in the castle, happily ever after.	Move DONKEY to far right. Move JACK to left of KING, PRINCESS to left of JACK. Put up MOTHER to left of PRINCESS, DONKEY to right of KING.

Follow-Up Activities

Questions for Discussion or Writing

1. Although Jack continued making mistakes, he kept on trying. Do you think he was really lazy? Why or why not? What things did Jack do that made him seem lazy?

2. Jack tried many different kinds of work. What work do you want to do someday? Where will you work? What will you do? Why did you choose that kind of work?

Game

Just Doing My Job

Display library books about careers. Have students write down the names of jobs that people do—farmer, teacher, lawyer, mechanic, cook, store clerk—one job on each slip of paper. Put all the slips of paper in a bag. Read aloud:

Each of you will draw one slip of paper and take a turn acting out the job in pantomime. While you are acting, you cannot say anything or make a sound. The rest of you who are not acting may guess what job the actor is doing. The one who guesses correctly may be the next actor or may choose who will have the next turn to act.

Recommended Read-Aloud Books on Related Topics

Stories about Being Different

Hoban, Russel. *Best Friends for Frances*. New York: Harper, 1969.

Levine, Arthur A. *The Boy Who Drew Cats: A Japanese Folktale*. New York: Dial, 1994.

Noble, Trina Hakes. *Meanwhile Back at the Ranch*. New York: Dial, 1987.

Sachar, Louis. *Marvin Redpost: Alone in His Teacher's House*. New York: Random House, 1994.

The Spindle, the Shuttle, and the Needle

Introduction

"The Spindle, the Shuttle, and the Needle" is one of the least familiar tales collected by the Brothers Grimm. It is a tale with a moral of virtue and hard work rewarded.

Before presenting the story, you might want to explore with the children the way clothing and cloth home furnishings are made. Have them look at a piece of cloth with a magnifying glass; a plaid pattern shows the woven threads most clearly. Let them look at and feel the seams of several cloth garments (not knits) as well as pillowcases and a curtain or bedspread. Point out the way the pieces of cloth are joined together with thread, especially on the hems and top edges of a dress or dressy trousers.

You might want to use a book such as Ali Mitgusch's *From Cotton to Pants* or *From Sheep to Scarf*, both published by Carolrhoda Books in 1984, to explain to the children the way people used the three tools named in the story's title to make clothing by these old methods. Display the felt figures of the wheel and spindle, the shuttle, and the needle on the flannelboard, and explain their uses. The spindle holds the thread as it is spun from fibers, either on a spinning wheel or by hand; the shuttle moves the

threads to weave them into cloth; the needle sews the cloth into clothing or home furnishings.

Set-Up Instructions

Set up the following figures on the flannelboard:

    9. Rich House (exterior view), centered vertically, a few inches from the left

    7. Cottage (interior view), centered vertically, a few inches from the right

Set up figures on the table, left to right:

   14. Woman [girl character in this tale]

   16. Woman [godmother character]

   64, 64a, 64b, 64c. Spinning Wheel with Spindle attached, Shuttle, Needle

   18, 18a. Man [prince character] with Crown

   15. Woman [young woman character]

   67. Carpet

   68. Curtains

   69. Cushion

   70. Pillow

    2. Distant Castle

Read Aloud

SCRIPT	FLANNELBOARD
Once upon a time there was a girl whose mother and father were dead. All her life she had lived in a cottage with her godmother, who earned her living making clothes.	**Put up GIRL to right of bed in COTTAGE, GODMOTHER to left of bed.**
The godmother taught the girl to use the spindle to spin fibers into thread, to use the shuttle to weave thread into cloth, and to use the needle to sew cloth into clothes. All through the years the girl and her godmother worked hard to make their living, and they were happy.	**Put up WHEEL to right of chair, SHUTTLE to left below WHEEL, NEEDLE to left of chair.**
When the girl was fifteen years old, her godmother became very ill. She called the girl to her bedside, and told her, "My dear, I feel that I am going to die. But you will be fine. I leave you this house to shelter you from wind and rain. I leave you the spindle, the shuttle, and the needle to clothe you and to earn your keep throughout your life. You are strong, my dear, and you will be fine."	**Move GODMOTHER to bed, lying down.**
For many years after her godmother died, the girl continued to live in her little cottage and to work hard spinning, weaving, and sewing. She earned just barely enough money to live, so she was very poor. The girl loved her work, but she was lonely and wanted to get married.	**Take down GODMOTHER. Move GIRL to chair.**
One fine spring, the prince was traveling through every town and village, looking for a woman to be his bride. Some people advised him to marry the richest girl, while others told him to marry the poorest girl of all. So in each town, the prince looked for both the poorest and the richest girl to see who would be the best wife for him.	**Put up PRINCE at far left top.**
One day the prince came to the village where the spinning, weaving, and sewing girl lived. First, he went to the home of the richest girl in town. She was standing outside her beautiful, rich house, dressed in her prettiest clothes, waiting for the prince to see her. When he saw her, he kept right on going.	**Move PRINCE down to left of RICH HOUSE.** **Put up YOUNG WOMAN to right of RICH HOUSE.** **Move PRINCE to right of YOUNG WOMAN. Take down YOUNG WOMAN.**
The prince went all the way out to the edge of town to the home of the poor sewing girl. She was spinning when the prince arrived. Although she saw the prince watching her, the girl continued to work, and she pretended not to see him. After awhile he passed by the cottage.	**Move PRINCE to right below COTTAGE.**

The girl's mind was not on the work in her hand after she had seen the handsome prince. As she spun the thread, she sang, "Spindle, spindle, spin so free; bring a wooer here to me."

Like magic, the spindle, trailing a golden thread, flew off the wheel and sped away from the cottage. It tapped the prince on the shoulder. Astounded to see a spindle moving along by itself, he began to follow the golden thread back toward its source.

Move SPINDLE down to PRINCE's shoulder.

Unable to spin without her spindle, the girl began to weave some cloth. As she plied the shuttle back and forth, back and forth, she sang in rhythm with her work: "Shuttle, shuttle, weave some more; bring my suitor to my door."

Move SHUTTLE to GIRL's hand.

Like magic, the shuttle flew from her hand, and it began to weave rapidly in front of the door. In no time at all, the magic shuttle had woven a beautiful carpet by the door—a carpet fit for a king or a princess.

Move SHUTTLE to left of COTTAGE.

Put up CARPET below SHUTTLE.

Finally, the girl picked up her needle and began to sing, "Needle, needle, sew and roam; fit this for a bridegroom's home."

Move NEEDLE to GIRL's hand.

Like magic, the needle flew all around the house. At the window, it sewed elegant curtains. At the bed, the needle sewed a lovely pillow fit for royalty to rest its head. Then the needle moved to the very chair where the girl had been sitting. She jumped up, and the needle made a soft cushion for the chair. Then it jumped back into the girl's hand, which is where it was when the prince arrived at the door to the cottage.

Move NEEDLE to window; put up CURTAIN.

Move NEEDLE to bed; put up PILLOW.

Move GIRL to left of COTTAGE; put up CUSHION in chair.

Move NEEDLE to GIRL's hand. Move PRINCE and SPINDLE to left of GIRL.

The prince looked all around him, and he exclaimed, "I thought you were the poorest girl, but your work has made a palace of this little house. You are both rich and poor, and you are the best bride for me."

Take down everything except PRINCE, GIRL, and NEEDLE.

The girl agreed to marry him. They left the little village and her little cottage, and they went to live in the prince's beautiful castle. But they took with them the spindle, the shuttle, and the needle to keep forever.

Put up DISTANT CASTLE at top left. Move WHEEL, SPINDLE, and SHUTTLE to right of GIRL.

Follow-Up Activities

Questions for Discussion or Writing

1. The girl in the story enjoyed making things. What art or craft activities do you do or would you like to try? What things have you made? What materials do you use?

2. If you could make only one thing for your house, what would you make? How would you use it?

Game

Who Is Spinning, Weaving, or Sewing?

Have everyone sit in a circle except for one child who will be the Guesser. Read aloud:

> We will send the Guesser out of the room, and I will choose one of you in the circle to be the Leader. The Leader will pantomime the action of spinning, weaving, or sewing, and the others in the circle will perform the same action. I will invite the Guesser back into the room to stand in the center of the circle as you continue your actions. From time to time the Leader will change the pantomime to a different action—sewing, weaving, or spinning. As soon as you see the Leader change the

action, the rest of you change in the same way. The Guesser may guess three times who is the Leader. If a guess is correct, the Guesser chooses the next Guesser. If all the guesses are wrong, the Leader may choose the next Guesser.

Remember how, in the story, the poor girl watched the Prince while pretending not to be watching him? In this game, watch the Leader without seeming to watch.

Recommended Read-Aloud Books on Related Topics

Stories about Wishing

Bond, Felicia. *Poinsettia and Her Family.* New York: Crowell, 1981.

Coombs, Patricia. *The Magic Pot.* New York: Lothrop, Lee & Shepard, 1977.

Oughton, Jerrie. *The Magic Weaver of Rugs: A Tale of the Navajo.* Boston: Houghton Mifflin, 1994.

Steig, William. *Sylvester and the Magic Pebble.* New York: Windmill, 1969.

Williams, Barbara. *Someday, Said Mitchell.* New York: Dutton, 1976.

Spider's Tug-of-War

Introduction

Throughout the world people tell trickster tales. The tricksters use their cunning words and crafty actions to get what they want from other characters. In western African countries and in the West Indies, people tell folktales about Spider or Ananse. In some stories Spider is a wise counselor, while in others he is a clever trickster.

Before presenting "Spider's Tug-of-War," you might want to share some library books about the countries of western Africa and about the islands of the West Indies. Find out what kinds of animals live in these places. Some of those animals will appear in this story about Spider.

Set-Up Instructions

Set up the following figures on the flannelboard:

6. Forest, vertically centered at the left

71. Sun, top center

8. Water [river in this tale], vertically centered at the right

Set up figures on the table, left to right:

42. Spider

41. Elephant

80, 4d. Basket with Shock of Wheat

43. Hippopotamus

44. Fish

65. Rope (with knot near center)

72. Moon

Read Aloud

In the great forest and along the great river, there was a great famine in all the land. All the animals were hungry. Spider was the most worried about his family. They had eaten all the food that was stored in their home near the river, and they were hungry. Spider thought and thought, until he thought of a plan to save his family.

Put up SPIDER in center.

First Spider walked into the forest until he came to Elephant's home. Spider said, "Good day, oh Lord of the Forest!"

Move SPIDER to below FOREST. Put up ELEPHANT to left of SPIDER.

Elephant was very suspicious of the old trickster. He replied, "What do you want?"

Spider said, "I come as a poor messenger to such a powerful beast as yourself. The Lord of the River, Hippopotamus, sends a message that he has a great longing for some of the wheat that you have stored in your home. His longing is so great, that in exchange for a basket of wheat brought to the river now, Hippopotamus will give you a large and powerful horse at harvest time, a horse worthy of you, oh Lord of the Forest."

Elephant replied, "A wonderful horse in exchange for a basket of wheat! That is an offer I cannot refuse!" So immediately he brought out a basket of wheat from his hidden food supply, and he carried it to the edge of the river to the place Spider showed him.

Put up BASKET of WHEAT on ELEPHANT's back.

Move ELEPHANT and BASKET of WHEAT to right of SPIDER.

Elephant looked all around. "Where is Hippopotamus?" he demanded. "I want to give him the wheat."

Spider answered, "In your great haste to make the exchange, I fear you have arrived at the river too early. But a great Lord of the Forest such as yourself should not have to wait for anyone. Let me, your humble servant, this mere messenger, wait here. I promise to speak to old Hippo on your behalf."

Gladly, Elephant returned to his home. As soon as he was gone, Spider carried the basket of wheat to his family's home, where they hid the wheat. Then he returned to the river with the empty basket.

Take down ELEPHANT.

Take down WHEAT.

Move SPIDER to below the RIVER and BASKET to right of SPIDER.

Spider did not have to wait very long until he saw Hippopotamus emerge from the water and begin to walk toward him. When Hippo saw Spider, he snorted, "What do you want, old trickster?"

Put up HIPPO to right of BASKET.

SCRIPT	FLANNELBOARD

Spider replied, "Good day, oh Lord of the River! I come as a humble messenger from the Lord of the Forest."

At first Hippopotamus was suspicious of the sly old spider. But when Spider came closer, Hippo saw that Spider did indeed have Elephant's own basket, so he listened carefully to the message from his old friend.

Spider said, "The Lord of the Forest has a great longing for some of your fresh fish, oh Lord of the River. In exchange for filling his basket with fish today, he has offered to give you a large, powerful horse at harvest time, a horse worthy of you, oh Lord of the River."

Hippopotamus lost no time in carrying the basket to the river, and he filled it to the brim with fresh fish. Spider moved just as fast, but he carried the basket of fish to his family. They built a fire to smoke the fish, so it would stay fresh for a long time.

Move HIPPO and BASKET to above RIVER. Put up FISH in BASKET.

Take down BASKET of FISH.
Take down HIPPO.

The fish and the wheat lasted for a long time. Spider's family ate well all through that season.

Move SPIDER to center.

Every day, Spider gathered vines from the forest, and his family worked at braiding and weaving the vines into a long, strong rope. When harvest time arrived, the rope was ready for the second part of Spider's plan.

Put up ROPE above SPIDER.

Take down ROPE.

The first to complain was Hippopotamus. He called out to Spider, "Hey, trickster! Where is my horse? I'm going to go ask Elephant about it right now!"

Put up HIPPO to right of SPIDER.

Spider replied, "Elephant just sent me here with a message for you. Come back here tomorrow morning, and your horse will be waiting for you in this very spot." Hippo went home happy.

Take down HIPPO.

Next Spider saw Elephant crashing through the forest. Elephant bellowed, "Where's my horse? It's harvest time, and I'm going to ask Hippo for him now."

Put up ELEPHANT to left of SPIDER.

Spider answered, "No need to worry, Lord of the Forest. I was just on my way to tell you to return to this very spot tomorrow morning to claim your fine horse." So Elephant went home happy also.

Take down ELEPHANT and SUN. Put up MOON.

SCRIPT	FLANNELBOARD
All during the night Spider was very busy. He stretched out the long vine-rope from the spot where he had talked to Elephant, all the way through the forest, to the spot where he had talked to Hippopotamus. But in the very middle, where it could not be seen from either end, Spider tied the vine-rope to a strong tree. Then he waited by the river for the day to begin.	**Put up ROPE from FOREST to RIVER.** **Move ROPE so knot is on a tree.** **Take down MOON. Put up SUN.**
He did not have long to wait until Hippopotamus hurried up to him. "Where's my horse?" he asked.	**Put up HIPPO at right end of ROPE.**
Spider replied, "Your horse is at the other end of this long rope. Oh, he is a *powerful* horse! But he is asleep. Let me go wake him very gently, so he won't shy away. When he is awake, I will pull two times on this rope, and you pull him in. Pull as hard as you can, for he is a big, strong horse!"	
So Hippo waited eagerly at his end of the vine-rope, while Spider hurried to the other end.	**Move SPIDER to left of FOREST.**
Elephant arrived the same time as Spider. Elephant said, "I want my horse! Where is it?"	**Put up ELEPHANT at left end of ROPE.**
Spider said, "At the other end of this rope, of course. But the horse is asleep. Just let me go wake him up, and I'll pull twice on the rope as a signal. Then you pull in the giant horse, just as hard as you can pull."	
Elephant waited at his end of the rope, while Spider hurried back to the hidden spot in the middle. He jerked twice on the rope, on both sides of the tree, and he saw the rope tighten as Elephant and Hippo began to pull.	**Move SPIDER to below knot, with two top legs touching ROPE.**
Spider went home, and he shared a good meal of fish and wheat with his family. Then he took a long nap, and he ate another big meal. Just as night fell, he walked back to his hidden spot in the middle of the vine-rope. "This has gone on long enough," he laughed as he cut the rope where it was tied to the tree.	**Take down SPIDER.** **Take down SUN; put up MOON. Put up SPIDER below knot, two top legs touching ROPE.**

SCRIPT	FLANNELBOARD

Spider listened, and after just a short time he heard a loud crash coming from both sides of him. First he jerked the two loose ends of the vine-rope toward him, and he hid them in the leaves of the forest floor. Then he ran quickly to the river, where he saw Hippopotamus lying on his back beside the water. Spider helped him to his feet, saying, "Whatever happened to you, oh Lord of the River? Why were you lying here in such an embarrassing position? Don't tell me that the *horse* knocked you off your feet!"

Take down ROPE.

Move HIPPO to far right, on his back. Move SPIDER to left of HIPPO.

Hippopotamus looked very embarrassed as Spider continued, "Where is the horse? And where is the rope?"

Hippopotamus looked all around, but he could not find any trace of the rope. Spider shook his head and asked, "What will Elephant say when he finds out that the Lord of the River could not hold his fine horse? Whatever will he say?"

Move HIPPO to standing position.

Hippopotamus begged, "Please, please, old friend, don't tell Elephant what happened. Don't ever say a word about this to anyone." So Spider promised never to tell about Hippo's lost horse.

Take down HIPPO.

Then Spider ran back to the forest. He found Elephant charging around, saying "Where is it? Where's my rope? Where is my beautiful horse? Did you see him?"

Move SPIDER to right of ELEPHANT.

Spider shook his head and answered, "No, I didn't see your horse, but I just saw Hippopotamus coming this way to see if you liked the fine horse he gave you. What will he say when he finds out you've already lost his gift?"

Elephant jumped up and began to run away. He turned back to Spider and called out, "Don't tell him! Don't tell him that you even saw me! Don't ever tell him what happened."

Spider promised never to tell Hippo what had happened to the horse. He laughed to himself as he said, "That is one promise that I plan to keep *always!*"

Take down ELEPHANT.

Follow-Up Activities

Questions for Discussion or Writing

1. Think of a second chapter for this story. One week later, Hippo and Elephant see each other at the edge of the river. What do they do? What do they say? If Spider hears them, what does he do?

2. Would you enjoy having a friend like Spider? Why or why not? What things about Spider would you like, and what would you dislike?

Activity

Tug-of-War

Scratch a line in the soil outdoors or mark a line indoors on the floor with masking tape. Divide the group into two teams, with each team on its own side of the line. Stretch a rope along the ground so that the center of the rope crosses the line. Instruct everyone to face the line on the ground and grip the rope with both hands. At the signal to begin, everyone will pull back until all the members of one team are pulled across the line.

Recommended Read-Aloud Books on Related Topics

Stories about Ananse

Kimmel, Eric A. *Anansi Goes Fishing.* New York: Holiday House, 1991.

Lester, Julius. *How Many Spots Does a Leopard Have? and Other Tales.* New York: Scholastic, 1989.

Stories about Spiders

Caduto, Michael J., and Joseph Bruchac. *Keepers of the Animals: Native American Stories and Wildlife Activities for Children.* Golden, Colo.: Fulcrum, 1991.

Stories about People in Africa

Brandenburg, Jim. *Sand and Fog: Adventures in Southern Africa.* New York: Walker, 1994.

Margolies, Barbara. *Olbalbal: A Day in Masailand.* New York: Four Winds, 1994.

Musgrove, Margaret. *Ashanti to Zulu.* New York: Dial, 1976.

Ward, Leila. *I Am Eyes: Ni Macho.* New York: Greenwillow, 1978.

The Little Red Hen

Introduction

This British tale is a favorite among teachers because the moral of the story emphasizes the value of hard work and dependability. It is such a well-known tale, people sometimes respond to a request to volunteer at work or at home with the refrain of " 'Not I,' said the _____ (dog, pig, rooster, etc.)." People unfamiliar with this story must wonder what in the world the speaker is implying.

The hen is a main character in two other folktales that people occasionally confuse with "The Little Red Hen." These are "Henny Penny" with its refrain of "The sky is falling!" and "The Cock, the Mouse, and the Little Red Hen" with a fox who captures the hen in a bag. Some confusion occurs because there are so many different versions of the story "The Little Red Hen," which is also called "The Little Red Hen and the Grain of Wheat." In various versions the animals include a frog, a dog, a pig, a cat, and a goose. But the refrains remain constant: " 'Not I,' said the _____ ," and "Then I will do it myself."

Before presenting this story, you might want to read about wheat in the encyclopedia. Read to find out how seeds are planted and what the plants look like as they grow. Read about or explain how wheat is harvested and what is done to separate the edible part from the rest of the plant.

Set-Up Instructions

Set up the following figures on the flannelboard:

6. Forest, centered vertically, far enough from left edge to allow for dog figure
5. Garden, centered on board with bottom of garden even with forest bottom edge
7. Cottage (interior view), at far right
71. Sun, top center
29. Hen, in basket in cottage

Set up figures on the table, left to right:

25. Dog
26. Cat
30. Rooster

22. Eggs
4d. Shock of Wheat
4. Seeds
72. Moon
47. Watering Can
4a. Seedlings
4b. Plants
4c. Wheat
55. Bowl
46. Bread
23. Hatching Chicks
24. Chicks

Read Aloud

SCRIPT	FLANNELBOARD
Early one morning out in the farmyard, all the animals were doing the same things they always did early in the morning. The hound dog found himself a nice, cool, shady spot under a tree to take a long nap until someone brought him his breakfast. The cat climbed up into a tree to sit perfectly still, waiting for a bird to come close enough to be caught for breakfast. The rooster sat on the ground, waiting for a juicy worm to come out of the ground for his breakfast. And the little red hen finished laying the last egg in her nest—an unusually large egg; she wondered if it might be twins—and went out into the garden to scratch up some food. She found a whole sheaf of ripe wheat, just full of seeds. She said, "Who will help me plant this wheat?"	**Put up DOG to left of FOREST.** **Put up CAT in tree of FOREST.** **Put up ROOSTER to right of FOREST.** **Put up EGGS below HEN (in basket).** **Move HEN to GARDEN; put up SHOCK in her beak.**
"Not I," said the dog.	
"Not I," said the cat.	
"Not I," said the rooster with a big yawn. "I have to get some rest so I can get up early tomorrow morning to crow."	**Turn ROOSTER onto back, feet up.**
So the little red hen answered, "Then I'll just have to plant the wheat myself." She worked hard all day under the hot sun, planting the wheat. When the sun went down, and night came on, she was very tired. She slept soundly all night long.	**Take down SHOCK. Put up SEEDS below GARDEN.** **Take down SUN; put up MOON. Move HEN to bed.**

When the sun came up the next morning, the rooster flew up to the roof, and he crowed very loudly to wake everyone up. The dog continued to sleep in the shade of the three. The cat continued to wait in the tree for a bird. The rooster sat down by the garden to see if the little red hen might scratch up something else to eat.

Take down MOON; put up SUN. Move ROOSTER to roof.

Move ROOSTER to right of FOREST.

The little red hen started working in her garden. She watered the ground, and she watched for weeds to sprout. She asked, "Who will help me pull these weeds?"

Move HEN to left of SEEDS; put up WATERING CAN in her beak.

Take down WATERING CAN.

"Not I," said the dog.

"Not I," said the cat.

"Not I," said the rooster, "I have to rest up from all my work early this morning."

Move ROOSTER to bed.

So the little red hen answered "Then I'll just have to pull all the weeds myself." So she did, working in the hot sun all day long. She pulled weeds and watered her garden every day.

The seeds grew into seedlings, and the seedlings grew into plants. Finally after many months, the wheat was tall, and its heads were ripe for harvesting. The little red hen asked, "Who will help me cut the wheat?"

Take down SEEDS; put up SEEDLINGS. Take down SEEDLINGS; put up PLANTS. Take down PLANTS; put up WHEAT.

"Not I," said the dog.

"Not I," said the cat.

"Not I," said the rooster. "Winter will be here soon, and I must enjoy this warm sunshine while it lasts. So he flew up into the tree and took a nap.

Move ROOSTER to tree.

So the little red hen answered, "Then I'll just have to cut all the wheat myself." And she did, cutting and carrying the ripe heads of wheat.

Take down WHEAT; put up SHOCK.

When all the wheat was cut, the little red hen said, "The good wheat needs to be separated from the chaff. Now who will help me thresh the wheat?"

"Not I," said the dog.

"Not I," said the cat.

SCRIPT	FLANNELBOARD
"Not I," said the rooster. "That wheat chaff makes me sneeze! I'm going to stay up here until the dust settles."	Move ROOSTER to roof.
So the little red hen said, "Then I'll just have to thresh all the wheat myself." And she did, working hard until her wings ached and her feet hurt and her beak was full of dust. But all the good wheat was separated from the chaff.	Take down SHOCK; put up BOWL below GARDEN.
By now it was nighttime again, and the little red hen was very tired. She went to sleep as soon as her head hit the pillow, and she didn't wake up until she heard the rooster crowing, "The sun is up! The sun is up!"	Take down SUN; put up MOON. Move HEN to bed, feet up.
	Take down MOON; put up SUN.
The little red hen got up too, and she began to call out, "Bread-baking day! Who will help me bake the bread?"	Move HEN to left of BOWL.
"Not I," said the dog.	
"Not I," said the cat.	
"Not I," said the rooster. "I'm busy eating all the little bugs that fell off the wheat."	Move ROOSTER to GARDEN.
So the little red hen said, "Alright, then, I'll bake it all myself." So she did, grinding the wheat, and mixing and kneading and punching down the beautiful loaf of bread. When the loaf had risen, she set it above the fire to bake.	Move BOWL to table, HEN to left of table. Take down BOWL. Put BREAD on top of fireplace.
The dog said, "My, my, my, what's that delicious smell?"	Move DOG to below HEN.
The cat said, "Dear, dear, dear, what is that luscious aroma?"	Move CAT to chair.
And the rooster said, "I'm hungry. Let's eat."	Move ROOSTER to top of table.
So the little red hen said, "Who will help me eat my bread?"	
"I will!" said the dog.	
"I will!" said the cat.	
"I will!" said the rooster. "Hot dog, dig in!"	
But the little red hen said, "You did not help me plant the wheat. You did not help me tend the garden. You did not help me cut the wheat or thresh it or bake the bread. Now you will not help me eat the bread. This bread is for my new little baby chickies, who are just hatching out of the eggs. Who will eat Mama's good hot bread?"	Move BREAD to table. Take down EGGS; put up HATCHING CHICKS. Move HEN and BREAD to left of HATCHING CHICKS.

"Not I," said the dog, walking away.	**Take down DOG.**
"Not I," said the cat, leaving.	**Take down CAT.**
"Not I," said the rooster. "I can tell when I'm not wanted around here." And he left too.	**Take down ROOSTER.**
So the little red hen and her new baby chicks ate up all the good hot bread.	**Take down HATCHING CHICKS; put up CHICKS below table.**

Follow-Up Activities

Questions for Discussion or Writing

1. Who cooks the food at your house? What work do the members of your family do at home? What housework do you know how to do? Do you help with any jobs now? Which ones? What will you learn to do in the future?

2. Which animal characters in the story did you like best? Which did you like least? What did you like and dislike about them?

Activity

Research about Chickens

Read together in the encyclopedia or in library books to find out about real hens—where they lay their eggs, how they care for the eggs, how the chicks hatch, what they eat and drink, how they stay warm.

Recommended Read-Aloud Books on Related Topics

Stories about Friends and Enemies

Blume, Judy. *The Pain and the Great One.* Scarsdale, N.Y.: Bradbury, 1974.

Cohen, Barbara. *Make a Wish, Molly.* New York: Doubleday, 1994.

Czernecki, Stefan. *The Hummingbird's Gift.* New York: Hyperion, 1994.

Flora, James. *Sherwood Walks Home.* New York: Harcourt, 1966.

Gackenbach, Dick. *Claude the Dog: A Christmas Story.* New York: Seabury, 1974.

Guthrie, Donna W. *Nobiah's Well: A Modern African Folktale.* Nashville: Ideals, 1993.

Steig, William. *Doctor DeSoto.* New York: Farrar, Straus & Giroux, 1982.

Books about Growing Plants

Bunting, Eve. *Flower Garden.* San Diego: Harcourt, 1994.

Hausherr, Rosmarie. *What Food Is This?* New York: Scholastic, 1994.

Coyote
Catches
the Fox

Introduction

The coyote is a small American member of the wolf family that is frequently featured in stories told over the centuries and across North America from Canada to Mexico. Many Native American tribes have folktales about Coyote the Trickster, a character who always tricks other animals with cunning talk.

In this story, another trickster matches wits with Coyote. Before you present the story, ask children to think about a contest between a coyote and fox. Ask if they have ever heard the expression "as sly as a fox." Ask children which of the two animals they think will be trickier in the story.

At the end of this tale, the audience can help to conclude the story by making the sound of the coyote—a high, yipping howl. Have the children practice the sound aloud before you begin the story. Ask them to listen for the place at the very end of the story when Coyote howls, so they can make the sound with you.

Set-Up Instructions

Set up the following figures on the flannelboard:

    6. Forest, near left edge of flannelboard

    8. Water [stream], to right of center

    44. Fish, in water near left edge of water

    71. Sun, above water

Set up figures on the table, left to right:

    35. Coyote

    34. Fox

    72. Moon

    73. Reflected Moon

Read Aloud

It seemed to Coyote that everywhere he went, and everything he did, Fox was there to ruin it for him. When Coyote went swimming, he couldn't see the bottom of the stream bed because Fox had been swimming there ahead of him and muddied the water. Whenever Coyote waited at the bank of the stream to catch fish, he never caught any because Fox was waiting upstream, catching all the fish before they got down to Coyote.

Put up COYOTE in middle of STREAM.

Put up FOX across STREAM, to right of COYOTE.

Move COYOTE to rocks below STREAM.

Move FOX to left of STREAM, beside fish.

Because Coyote didn't have any fish, he grew hungry. So he dug into a rabbit burrow to try to catch a rabbit to eat. But Fox ruined that, too. Fox waited at the other end of the burrow to catch the rabbit when it ran away from Coyote's end of the burrow.

Move COYOTE to left of FOREST.

Move FOX to right of FOREST.

So Coyote got hungrier and hungrier. The hungrier he got, the angrier he felt. And the angrier he felt, the more he thought about how all his problems were really the fault of old Fox. Then Coyote felt even angrier at Fox than before.

Move COYOTE to far left.

When Coyote saw Fox standing under a tall tree, he was so angry that he just ran right over and jumped on Fox. Coyote yelled, "You've caused me too much trouble. But not anymore! I'm going to tear you apart."

Move COYOTE to top of FOX.

Fox slid away a little so that only his tail was still caught by Coyote, and he said, "Oh, alright, but could you please let me eat the prairie chickens first? Then when you kill me, I'll die happy."

Move FOX to right.

Coyote looked all around and said, "What prairie chickens? I don't see any prairie chickens."

Move COYOTE to left.

Fox said, "Oh, they'll be coming along any minute because I tricked them. I sent word that I was lying very ill under this tree, and the mother prairie chicken said she would bring me some good medicine here to make me well. Say, now, Coyote, if you're hungry, why don't you wait here with me, and you can eat some of the prairie chickens, too!"

Turn FOX over onto his back.

Coyote wanted to do that. He really was very hungry. But he said, "I don't see any prairie chickens around here. I don't think they're coming."

Turn COYOTE over onto his back.

Fox said, "Well, if they see you lying here, they probably won't come near. Why don't you hide up there in the top of that tree? Don't come down until the prairie chickens get here."

Turn COYOTE over to stand on hind legs.

SCRIPT	FLANNELBOARD

So Coyote began to climb up the tree. It was hard work because he wasn't a very good climber. The rough bark of the tree hurt his paws and scraped his legs, but Fox kept calling out from below, "Higher, go higher, Coyote. I can still see you from down here. Climb up higher and hide."

Move COYOTE to tree trunk.
Move COYOTE to middle, then to top of tree.

So Coyote kept climbing until he was at the very top of the tree. Then he looked down to see if the prairie chickens were coming, but all he saw was the fox running away into the open countryside. Slowly and painfully Coyote climbed down out of the tree.

Move FOX to rocks below STREAM.
Move COYOTE to middle of tree, then down to right of FOREST.

Now Coyote was not a very good climber, but he was a pretty good runner. He was so angry that even on his sore paws he caught up with Fox. He was surprised to find Fox standing perfectly still and leaning against the side of a steep cliff. Fox said, "Careful, Coyote, don't let this cliff fall on you."

Move COYOTE to below FOX.
Turn FOX to stand on hind legs (with back leaning against the tan ground at the bottom edge of STREAM).

Coyote said, "What are you talking about, Fox? That cliff isn't falling down."

Fox said, "That's because I'm holding it up. I'm pushing really hard against this cliff. It's a big job. I don't know how much longer I can hold it up. I'm glad you came along to help."

Coyote said, "I'm not going to help you."

Fox said, "Then I guess we'll both get killed when I let go and the cliff falls on us." He started to move away.

Move FOX to right.

Coyote rushed over to the cliff, and he leaned hard against it. He asked, "How long am I going to have to stay here?"

Move COYOTE to lean on tan ground at bottom edge of STREAM.

SCRIPT	FLANNELBOARD
Fox answered, running off, "Just until I can bring back a big tree branch to prop up the falling cliff. Don't worry if I'm gone a long time. It may take awhile for me to find a branch big enough to hold that cliff."	**Move FOX to right.**
	Take down FOX.
Coyote leaned against the cliff and waited for a long time. He waited for such a long time that the sun went down and the moon came up. Finally he said, "My back hurts and my legs ache. I just can't hold up this cliff any longer. I'm going to have to let go."	**Take down SUN; put up MOON.**
He fell away from the cliff, and he closed his eyes, waiting for the crash. When time had passed and nothing had fallen down, Coyote knew that Fox had tricked him again. Now he was angrier and hungrier and thirstier than ever. He walked back to the stream to get a drink of water. He was very surprised to see Fox standing up on the bank of the stream, watching him. Coyote yelled, "Now what are you doing?"	**Move COYOTE to right.** **Move COYOTE to left of STREAM.** **Put up FOX on grass above STREAM.**
Fox answered, "I had baked a lovely cornbread to share with you, but now I won't be able to."	
Coyote said, "Why can't you give me some of your cornbread?"	**Turn COYOTE to stand on hind legs.**
Fox said, "Because I dropped your piece in the stream. Look down there, and you can see it in the water."	**Turn FOX to point into STREAM.**
So Coyote looked, and there deep in the water he saw a slice of something kind of white. It looked like a slice of cornbread.	**Put up REFLECTED MOON in STREAM.**
Coyote jumped right into that stream, and he started biting at the white thing he saw in the water. He bit and he swallowed, and he took in a lot of water.	**Move COYOTE into STREAM.**
Fox called out, "Get it, Coyote! Get that slice of cornbread. Don't give up until you've swallowed all the water so you can pick up your cornbread from the stream bed."	
So Coyote bit and swallowed more and more and more until he was so full of water he could barely move, but he never did find that piece of cornbread in the stream.	

When Coyote finally looked up to see why Fox wasn't speaking to him anymore, all he saw was the moon rising high into the sky—the moon that reflected on the still surface of the water in the stream. That's when he knew that Fox had tricked him once again. Coyote was so upset and angry and sore and still hungry that he raised his nose toward the moon and called . . . (howl and yip).

Take down FOX.

Turn COYOTE to stand on hind legs.

Follow-Up Activities

Questions for Discussion or Writing

1. Who was smarter, Coyote or Fox? What were the best decisions that each of them made?

2. If Coyote wanted to play a trick on Fox, what could he do? What would Fox do then?

Activity

Sequencing Events

Ask two or three students who write well to come to the chalkboard and record sentences as the class says them. Read aloud:

In the story, Fox did six things that bothered Coyote. Think of the things Fox did. Say each thing in a sentence. (Example: Fox told Coyote to climb the tree and hide.) (After all six sentences are written) Let's number the sentences in the same order Fox did those things in the story. What happened first? Second?

After the sentences are numbered, choose volunteers to act out the story as the class reads the sentences aloud in unison and in numerical order.

Recommended Read-Aloud Books on Related Topics

Story about a Fox

Mason, Cherie. *Wild Fox: A True Story.* Camden, Maine: Down East Books, 1993.

Stories about Coyote

Johnston, Tony. *The Tale of Rabbit and Coyote.* New York: Putnam, 1994.

Oughton, Jerrie, *How the Stars Fell into the Sky: A Navajo Legend.* Boston: Houghton Mifflin, 1992.

Stevens, Janet. *Coyote Steals the Blanket: A Ute Tale.* New York: Holiday House, 1993.

Stories about Other Tricksters

Hadithi, Mwenye. *Tricky Tortoise.* Boston: Little, Brown, 1988.

Knutson, Barbara. *Sungara and Leopard: A Swahili Trickster Tale.* Boston: Little, Brown, 1993.

Little Red Riding Hood

Introduction

"Little Red Riding Hood" is one of the best-known European folktales. It gives us the character of the Big Bad Wolf, as he is called in the English story "The Three Little Pigs." In many of the modern adaptations of this tale presented in books or film, the wolf does not eat Grandmother or the little girl, and the woodcutter does not kill the wolf.

This flannelboard adaptation of the story is based on the version recorded by the Brothers Grimm. When you present this story, if you prefer to expurgate the violence of the grandmother and Little Red Riding Hood being eaten and of the wolf being slain, you can substitute your own words for the underlined phrases. For example, you can say that the wolf locked Grandmother and Little Red Riding Hood in the closet for a later snack, and the woodcutter scared the wolf away to rescue them. Whichever version you use, the placement and removal of the felt figures on the flannelboard will be the same.

Set-Up Instructions

Set up the following figures on the flannelboard:

6. Forest, to the left of center

7. Cottage (interior view), to the right of center

Set up figures on the table, left to right:

16. Woman [Grandmother character in this tale]

13. Girl [Little Red Riding Hood character]

16a. Cap

35. Wolf

75. Bouquet

20. Man [woodcutter character]

76. Hatchet (in woodcutter's hand)

Read Aloud

Once upon a time, far away in a deep, dark woods, there stood a little cottage. In this cottage there lived an old woman. She had made a pretty red hood for her granddaughter, whom she loved very much. Since the granddaughter wore the red hood all the time, everyone called her "Little Red Riding Hood."

Put up GRANDMOTHER to right of bed. Put up RED RIDING HOOD to left of FOREST.

One day the grandmother was feeling ill, so Little Red Riding Hood's mother baked some bread as a gift. As Little Red Riding Hood set out to walk to her grandmother's house, she remembered what her mother had told her, "Take this basket of bread to your sick grandmother. And mind you go directly to her house. Do not stop along the way."

Move GRANDMOTHER to bed; put up CAP on her head.

Move RED RIDING HOOD down.

So Little Red Riding Hood started to walk directly through the woods to her grandmother's house. She had not gone very far when she met a big gray wolf. Little Red Riding Hood said to the wolf, "Hello, kind sir. Who are you?"

Move RED RIDING HOOD to right, below FOREST.

Put up WOLF to left of RED RIDING HOOD.

Very surprised, the wolf answered, "I'm a big w . . . I mean a good friend. And where are you going today, little girl?"

Little Red Riding Hood said, "I'm going to my sick grandmother's house to take her this bread," for she did not know the wolf, and she was not frightened of him.

Looking at the bread made the wolf hungry, so he licked his lips and said, "Does your grandmother live far away?"

Little Red Riding Hood answered, "Oh, no, she lives in that little cottage just on the other side of the woods."

The wolf looked at the cottage, and he thought of a wicked plan that would give him two people to eat for his dinner. "Oh, just look at those pretty flowers," said the wolf. "It's a shame that your grandmother doesn't have some of those flowers to make her feel better."

Move WOLF up, to left of flowers on FOREST.

Little Red Riding Hood began to pick the flowers, just as the wolf had known she would. Every time she picked one flower and put it in her basket, she saw another one even prettier, so she walked farther and farther into the woods.

Move RED RIDING HOOD up.

Put up BOUQUET in basket.

Meanwhile, the wolf ran directly to Grandmother's cottage. He knocked on the door. Grandmother called out in a weak voice, "Who's there?"

Move WOLF to left below COTTAGE.

The wolf answered, changing his voice to try and sound like a little girl, "It is I, Little Red Riding Hood. I've brought you a present, Grandmother."

The old woman answered, "The door is not locked, my dear; just lift the latch and come right in. The wolf rushed into the room, and he ate the old woman up. He swallowed her whole, before she even had a chance to scream! Then he put on Grandmother's cap, and he lay in wait in her bed.

> **Move WOLF up. Take down GRANDMOTHER.**
>
> **Move WOLF to bed; put up CAP on his head.**

Soon Little Red Riding Hood arrived at her grandmother's cottage. She knocked on the door. Changing his voice to sound like the old woman, the wolf said, "Who's there?"

> **Move RED RIDING HOOD to left below COTTAGE.**

Little Red Riding Hood answered, "It is I, Little Red Riding Hood. I've brought you a present, Grandmother."

Again the wolf answered, changing his voice, "The door is not locked, my dear; just lift the latch and come right in."

So Little Red Riding Hood lifted the latch, and she walked into the cottage. She looked at the wolf lying on the bed, and she thought that Grandmother looked very different today. She said, "Oh, Grandmother, what big feet you have!"

> **Move RED RIDING HOOD to right of bed.**

And the wolf answered in his old woman's voice, "The better to hurry to you with, my dear."

When the wolf said that, the cap slipped off away from his eyes, and Little Red Riding Hood exclaimed, "Oh, Grandmother, what big eyes you have!"

> **Take down CAP.**

And the wolf answered, "The better to see you with, my dear!"

When the wolf said that, he opened his mouth very wide, and Red Riding Hood exclaimed, "Oh, Grandmother! What big teeth you have!"

The wolf roared, "The better to eat you with!" And he swallowed Red Riding Hood whole, hood and all!

> **Take down RED RIDING HOOD.**

After eating such a big meal, the wolf felt very full and very sleepy. So he lay back down on Grandmother's bed, fell fast asleep, and snored.

> **Turn WOLF over, onto his back.**

SCRIPT	FLANNELBOARD
He snored so loud that a woodcutter who had been working in the forest heard the snores as he was passing by. The woodcutter said, "I've known that old woman for a long time, but I've never heard her snore that loud before. Maybe I'd better see if something is wrong."	**Put up WOODCUTTER between FOREST and COTTAGE.** **Take down HATCHET.**
Very quietly the woodcutter peeked through the open door. When he saw the wolf asleep in the bed, he guessed that the wolf might have eaten the old woman. As the wolf slept soundly, the woodcutter took out his knife and split open the wolf's belly. Imagine his surprise when the first thing he saw inside was the little red hood! Red Riding Hood came out, alive but scared, followed by her poor grandmother, who felt even sicker now than she had before.	**Move WOODCUTTER to left below COTTAGE.** **Move WOODCUTTER to left of bed.** **Put up RED RIDING HOOD below bed to right. Put up GRANDMOTHER below bed to left.**
While the wolf still slept, Red Riding Hood and the woodcutter filled the hole in the wolf's belly with big, heavy rocks. When the wolf awoke and tried to run away, the heavy rocks made him fall off the bed to the floor, where he died.	**Move RED RIDING HOOD up to right of bed.**
So the woodcutter took home the wolf's fur, and Grandmother ate the bread and felt better. Red Riding Hood decided to walk right straight home and never stop in the woods again.	**Take down WOLF and WOODCUTTER.** **Move RED RIDING HOOD down.**

Follow-Up Activities

Questions for Discussion or Writing

1. What is the safety rule about talking to strangers? When Little Red Riding Hood met the wolf in the forest, what could she have done? If she had done that, how would the story have ended differently?

2. What is the safety rule about locking and answering the door when you are home alone? When the wolf knocked on Grandmother's door, what should she have done? How would the story have ended then?

3. In this story, the wolf is supposed to be very big and very, very bad. Read about wolves in the encyclopedia. How big are they? Where do they live? What do they eat? Are they truly evil creatures?

Game

Changing Your Voice

With children seated facing you, read aloud:

When the wolf talked to Grandmother, he changed his voice to sound like Little Red Riding Hood. Can you change your voice to sound like someone else? In this game one child will be Grandmother, who sits in a chair at the front of the room facing away from the other children. Another child will be the wolf, who knocks on a table. Grandmother will ask, "Who's there?" and the wolf must answer, "It is I, Little Red Riding Hood. I have brought you a present," in a voice different from his usual. Grandmother must guess who is really speaking. If Grandmother guesses correctly, she chooses who will be the next Grandmother. If she guesses incorrectly, the wolf may play the next Grandmother.

Little Red Riding Hood **135**

Recommended Read-Aloud Books on Related Topics

Stories about Escaping from Danger

dePaola, Tomie. *Fin McCoul: The Giant of Knockmany Hill.* New York: Holiday House, 1981.

Gackenbach, Dick. *Harry and the Terrible Whatzit.* New York: Seabury, 1977.

Stories about Solving a Problem

Henkes, Kevin. *A Weekend with Wendell.* New York: Greenwillow, 1986.

Slobodkina, Esphyr. *Caps for Sale.* New York: HarperCollins, 1947, 1987.

Books about Wolves

Allard, Harry. *It's So Nice to Have a Wolf around the House.* Garden City, N.Y.: Doubleday, 1977.

Brandenberg, Jim. *To the Top of the World.* New York: Walker, 1993.

The Musicians of Bremen Town

Introduction

Although the setting of this story is obviously Germany (Bremen is a real town), the tale has traveled. A story with substantially the same plot, "The Animal Musicians," appears in Ricardo E. Alegría's book *The Three Wishes: A Collection of Puerto Rican Folktales.*

Much of the appeal of this story is the "singing" of the animals. Let the children help you make the sounds. Before you present the story, practice having the students make the specified sound when you point to the animal figure on the flannelboard. When you point to the donkey, they say, "Hee-haw"; the dog, "aaa-ooh"; the cat, "meow, row"; and the rooster, "cock-a-doodle-doo." During the presentation of the story, whenever you want the children to make an animal sound, point to the felt figure.

Set-Up Instructions

Set up the following figures on the flannelboard:

57. Sign, at the extreme left edge just below vertical center

6. Forest, near the bottom and left of center

7. Cottage (exterior view), in top right corner

71. Sun, top center

Set up figures on the table, left to right:

31. Donkey
25. Dog
26. Cat
30. Rooster
72. Moon
20. Man [old robber character in this tale]
17. Woman [woman robber character]
18. Man [young robber character]

Read Aloud

———————— SCRIPT ————————   ———— FLANNELBOARD ————

It was early morning, but the old donkey was already feeling tired. He sat down at the side of the road and moaned, "Life is not fair! Why should an old donkey like myself have to walk so far down this lonely road? I worked hard for years without complaining, carrying those heavy sacks of grain to the mill, day after day, year after year. Yet, now that I'm getting older, and I can't carry such heavy loads anymore, the farmer just turns me out to take care of myself. Well, I'll show him; I *can* take care of myself. I'll go to the town of Bremen, and I'll join their famous band. There was never a horn that could play so beautifully as my voice, hee-haw, hee-haw, hee-haw!"

Put up DONKEY on far left.

This loud braying might have gone on for a long time, if it hadn't been interrupted by a loud howl, "Aaa-ooh," coming from farther down the road.

Put up DOG (nose up) to right of DONKEY.

The donkey walked until he saw a hound dog with his nose pointed toward the sky, howling, "Aaa-ooh, ooh, ooh, ooh!"

The donkey asked him, "Why are you howling, old sad dog?"

The dog answered in a forlorn voice, "You'd howl, too, brother donkey, if your life was at an end. For years I served my master well, but now that my old nose can't sniff the scents so well on a hunt, my master will have me killed! Aaa-ooh!"

The donkey answered him, "Peace, old sad dog; there may be a solution to both our problems. With a voice like yours, you could join me in the Bremen town band! Come with me to Bremen." So the dog and the donkey set off together on the road to Bremen.

Move DONKEY and DOG just to left of FOREST.

They had not gone very far when they heard a caterwauling coming from high off the ground. They looked up into a tall tree and saw a cat shrieking, "Meow, row!"

Put up CAT in tree on left side of FOREST.

The donkey said, "Brother cat, what ails you? Never have I heard an angrier cry."

The cat replied, "Never have I heard of such treason. This morning I overheard my mistress say that just because I was too old to catch mice anymore, she was going to have me drowned! Well, I ran away at once and hid in this tree, but now I don't know what to do or where to go!"

The donkey said, "Perhaps we can help you, and you can turn your wailing to better use. Come with us on the road to Bremen. When we arrive, we'll join the town band together."

So the cat, the dog, and the donkey set out together down the road to Bremen. After awhile they stopped and lay down at the side of the road to take a little nap. They were awakened from their sleep by a rooster crowing, "Cock-a-doodle-doo!"

Move CAT to right side of DOG.

Put up ROOSTER to right of CAT.

The cat exclaimed angrily, "What is the meaning of this raucous interruption?"

The rooster told them, "Don't worry. You won't hear noise from me much longer. I heard the folks talking. Company's coming. They're going to eat a big supper. And *I'm* going to *be* the supper! Just thought I'd crow while I could." And he crowed again, "Cock-a-doodle-doo."

The donkey told him, "Peace to you, our brother, and take heart. With a voice like that, you are just the one to go with us to Bremen. Together we will join the town band."

So the rooster, the cat, the dog, and the donkey set off together down the road to Bremen. They walked all day, until the sun went down and night fell on the dark woods.

Take down SUN; put up MOON.

The rooster said, "Getting cold, isn't it?"

The cat said, "Never have I felt such hunger pangs."

The dog said, "It certainly is dark in these woods at night."

And the donkey said, "We need to find a place to eat and sleep tonight." All the animals looked at the donkey, but for once he did not have a solution to their problems.

Finally the cat climbed a tree, looked around, and said, "In the distance there appears a light."

Move CAT to top of tree on right side of FOREST.

The rooster said, "Now I see it too. Looks like a house."

The donkey said, "We should all go there and see if there is any food and shelter for us tonight."

SCRIPT	FLANNELBOARD
So the rooster, the cat, the dog, and the donkey all walked through the woods to the little house. The cat looked in through the window, while the other animals waited anxiously in the dark.	Move all animals to left of COTTAGE. Move CAT to window, then back down to left of COTTAGE.
They all asked, "What did you see?" as the cat jumped back down to the ground.	
The cat warned them, "Shhh! Never have I seen such mean-looking people as the three robbers inside this house! One man looks like a bandit, with a big, sharp knife! One of the robbers is a woman. And the last robber dresses all in fine, rich clothes."	Flip over COTTAGE. Put up OLD ROBBER in left side of COTTAGE. Put up WOMAN ROBBER to right of OLD ROBBER. Put up YOUNG ROBBER to right of WOMAN ROBBER.
The rooster exclaimed, "Must have robbed some rich folks, and he stole their clothes!"	
The dog asked, "Did the robbers have any food?"	
The cat answered, "Above the fire was a big kettle of hot soup. They were just about to dine."	
The dog moaned, "Oh, how I wish for just one bowl of their soup and a warm place by their fire!"	
The donkey said, "Sh! I have a plan. Listen." He whispered in each animal's ear. Then the donkey moved over to a spot just under the window. The dog climbed onto his back, the cat climbed onto the dog's back, and the rooster flew up to the top of the stack.	Move DONKEY to left of COTTAGE, DOG on DONKEY's back, CAT on DOG's back, ROOSTER on CAT's head.
The donkey counted, "One, two, three, go!" And they made the loudest noise; it sounded like "hee-haw," "aaah-ooh," "meow, row," and "cock-a-doodle-doo," all at the same time.	
The noise was so loud and so unexpected that the three robbers jumped up from the dinner table and ran off into the dark night without looking back even once.	Take down three ROBBERS.
The rooster ate all the corn he could find, and then he flew up to the roof to roost for the night. The cat went right into the cottage and ate a whole bowl of soup before he fell asleep in a chair. The dog carried his food to the bed, where he ate and then fell asleep. The donkey found plenty of hay to eat behind the cottage, so he ate until he was sleepy, too. All the animals were sleeping peacefully as the fire burned itself out.	Move ROOSTER to roof of COTTAGE. Move CAT to chair. Move DOG to bed. Move DONKEY to below COTTAGE.

SCRIPT	**FLANNELBOARD**
In the cold, dark woods the three robbers had finally stopped running. The first robber said, "What was that?"	**Put up OLD ROBBER to left of FOREST.**
The second robber said, "When you ran out, I just followed you. I didn't even see it."	**Put up WOMAN ROBBER to right of OLD ROBBER.**
The third robber said, "I don't know what it was either. Maybe we shouldn't have left."	**Put up YOUNG ROBBER to right of WOMAN ROBBER.**
Then the first robber said, "I'm going back there to see what's in our house. They can't scare *me* away!" And he walked straight back to the house.	**Move OLD ROBBER to left side of COTTAGE.**
When the robber arrived at the house, the fire had gone out, and everything was very dark. The cat opened his eyes, and the moonlight reflected off them. The robber thought the glowing eyes were glowing coals in the fireplace, so he walked closer to stir up the fire.	**Move OLD ROBBER to left of DOG. Move CAT to OLD ROBBER's head.**
The cat jumped onto the man's head with a loud yowl. The dog woke up, and bit the man on the leg. The man ran outside, where the donkey gave him a big kick that sent him flying back toward his friends, as the rooster crowed, "Cock-a-doodle-doo."	**Move DOG to OLD ROBBER's leg. Move OLD ROBBER down, then to left of FOREST.**
The other robbers asked him, "Why did you come running back so fast? What happened?"	
He answered, "Oh, it was awful! First a witch scratched me with her long fingernails. Then a man with a knife stabbed me in the leg. After that another man with a wooden club hit hard. And when I tried to run away, I heard a loud voice from on high call out, 'Come back, you!' I'm *never* going back there!"	
The three robbers ran away, and they were never seen near there again.	**Take down three ROBBERS.**
The four animal friends were so happy in their new home that they stayed right there for many a day. Although they never did make it to Bremen, they made their own music in the evenings. You might hear them someday, singing, "Hee-haw," "Aah-ooh," "Meow, row," and "Cock-a-doodle-doo," all at the same time.	**Take down MOON; put up SUN.**

Follow-Up Activities

Questions for Discussion and Writing

1. If the four animals had gone to the town of Bremen, what would have happened? What would they have said to the musicians in the town? Would the townspeople have welcomed them? Why or why not? Where would the animals have lived and worked?

2. When the robbers ran away, where do you think they went? How did they make a living after that? Should the animals have taken the robbers' food and house? Why or why not?

Dramatic Play

Animal Sounds

Divide the children into four groups and assign an animal to each group. Read aloud:

> Name the four animals in the story. Each group represents one of these animals. Let's hear how the animals' music sounded in the story. When I say the name of your group's animal, create the musical sound that your animal would make. (Practice each animal's sound.) Now we will sing a song together as an animal choir, with each group singing the song in its animal voice.

Recommended Read-Aloud Books on Related Topics

Books about Musicians

Duvoisin, Roger. *Petunia and the Song*. New York: Knopf, 1951.

London, Jonathan. *Hip Cat*. San Francisco: Chronicle, 1993.

Pinkney, Brian. *Max Found Two Sticks*. New York: Simon & Schuster, 1994.

Books about Being Different

Cannon, Janell. *Stellaluna*. San Diego: Harcourt, 1993.

Steig, William. *The Amazing Bone*. New York: Farrar, Straus & Giroux, 1976.

Zion, Gene. *Harry the Dirty Dog*. New York: Harper & Row, 1956, 1984.

Rapunzel

Introduction

Anyone familiar with European fairy tales would recognize the familiar refrain "Rapunzel, Rapunzel, let down thy hair." Filled with acts of violence, jealousy, and vindictiveness, this story can be very scary. You may find that it is more suitable for older school-age children rather than preschool or even kindergarten and first-grade students.

Before presenting this story, explain to the children that "rampion" ("rapunzel" in German) is the name of a vegetable similar to a turnip. It has green leaves and blue flowers, and the raw white roots are eaten in salads.

Set-Up Instructions

Set up the following figures on the flannelboard:

    7. Cottage (interior view), near left edge

  71. Sun, top center

Set up figures on the table, left to right:

  19. Man [husband character in this tale]

  14. Woman [wife character]

  5, 81, 81a. Garden with Two Rampions and One Rampion

  72. Moon

  17. Woman [old woman character]

  12. Baby

  15. Woman [Rapunzel character]

   6. Forest

   3, 3a. Tower (folded) with Door

15a. Hair

  18, 18a. Man [prince character] with Crown

  65. Rope

   2. Distant Castle

Read Aloud

SCRIPT	FLANNELBOARD
Once upon a time a husband and wife lived in a cottage, and they were expecting their first baby. They were very happy about the baby that would be coming soon.	**Put up HUSBAND and WIFE to left of COTTAGE.**
Next to the cottage there was a garden full of lovely rampions, which the wife liked to eat in her salads. She looked at all those rampions, and she hungered for some to eat. The more she looked at the rampions, the hungrier she became. The hungrier she became, the more she looked at the rampions.	**Put up GARDEN with TWO RAMPIONS and ONE RAMPION to right of COTTAGE.**
Her husband said, "Oh, don't even look at those rampions. You know that the garden belongs to a wicked old woman, and she does horrible things to anyone who dares to enter her garden."	
But all during the night, the wife kept looking at the rampions through the window until she made herself sick with wanting them so much.	**Take down SUN; put up MOON. Move WIFE to bed.**
The husband did not want his wife to be sick, so he decided to creep into the dark garden to get some of the rampions. He sneaked into the garden and picked some rampions, and then he sneaked back out again without being caught.	**Move HUSBAND to left of GARDEN. Move TWO RAMPIONS to his hand; move HUSBAND and TWO RAMPIONS to left of WIFE.**
The next morning the wicked old woman went for a walk in her garden. She saw that some of her rampions were missing, and it made her very angry. She cried, "Who dared to come into my garden last night and steal my rampions? I'll find out who the thief is. Tonight I'll hide in the garden, and I'll catch him."	**Take down MOON; put up SUN. Put up OLD WOMAN in GARDEN.**
Back in the cottage, the wife had eaten all the rampions, and she had enjoyed them very much. All day she kept thinking about how good they were, and she asked her husband to bring her some more. She said, "You didn't get caught before, and you won't get caught this time."	**Move OLD WOMAN to behind tall bush in GARDEN.** **Take down TWO RAMPIONS.**
The husband was afraid, and he did not want to go back in the wicked woman's garden. But again his wife was making herself sick with wanting some rampions, so he decided to go back into the old woman's garden another time.	

SCRIPT	FLANNELBOARD
As soon as it got dark that night, the husband sneaked into the garden. He did not know that the wicked old woman was watching from behind the clump of bushes. Quietly the man crept up to the patch of rampions. Just as he put out his hand to pull up a bunch of rampions, he heard a voice call out, "Stop, thief! Now I've caught you. I'll make you pay for your thievery."	**Take down SUN; put up MOON. Move HUSBAND to GARDEN.**
	Move OLD WOMAN to left of HUSBAND.
The husband was very frightened. He begged, "Oh, please, my wife is expecting a baby, and she wanted some rampions to eat. She craved them until she got sick. I only took them for her sake."	
With an evil smile on her face, the wicked old woman said, "So your wife is going to have a baby, eh? Well then, you just take that rampion for her. But it has its price. Yes, its price is the child itself. When the child is twelve years old, it is mine."	**Take down OLD WOMAN.**
The man grabbed the rampion and ran from the garden. He did not tell his wife what the old woman had said, because he did not really believe that the woman would ever take their child.	**Move HUSBAND and ONE RAMPION to left of WIFE.**
Many weeks went by. The husband and wife were very happy when their baby girl was born. On the day the child was born, the old woman came to see her. She told the husband and wife to call the child "Rapunzel" because of the rampions that they had taken from her garden.	**Take down MOON. Take down ONE RAMPION. Put up BABY in basket.** **Put up OLD WOMAN to left below COTTAGE.** **Take down OLD WOMAN.**
Rapunzel grew older and was a happy child. Her father did not worry about the old woman's threat as the child grew up through the years. On Rapunzel's twelfth birthday, while her parents were out of the house, she saw an old woman coming from the garden next door. Rapunzel had never heard about the wicked old woman, so she was not afraid. The old woman invited Rapunzel to come with her to see her beautiful garden. Although Rapunzel's parents had told her never to go near the garden, she was curious to see it, and she went with the old woman.	**Take down BABY. Put up RAPUNZEL on right side of COTTAGE. Take down HUSBAND and WIFE.** **Put up OLD WOMAN to right of RAPUNZEL.**
The old woman and Rapunzel walked in the garden for a long time. Rapunzel became tired, and she wanted to go back home. But the old woman grabbed her by the arm and walked past the garden into the forest with her. They walked for a long time into the deep, dark forest, so far that Rapunzel could not see her home anymore.	**Move RAPUNZEL and OLD WOMAN to right of GARDEN.** **Move OLD WOMAN closer to RAPUNZEL, touching her arm.** **Take down GARDEN; put up FOREST.** **Take down COTTAGE.**

SCRIPT	FLANNELBOARD
When they reached the other side of the woods, Rapunzel was so tired that she did not think she could walk any farther. Finally, they reached a tall tower. The wicked old woman made Rapunzel climb up the stairs to the very top of the tower. She put some food and water inside. Then she closed the door and sealed it shut, so that no one could enter or leave the tower.	Move FOREST to left. Put up TOWER with DOOR to right of FOREST. Move RAPUNZEL to behind TOWER, head visible through window. Take down DOOR.
Rapunzel stayed in the tower all alone. Her hair grew very, very long. Every day the old woman brought her water and food. When she arrived at the tower, the woman would stand under the window and call, "Rapunzel, Rapunzel, let down thy hair." Then Rapunzel would unwind her long, long hair, wrap it around a hook on the windowsill, and let it hang down outside the window. The old woman would climb up Rapunzel's hair like a ladder and bring her some food for the day.	Put up HAIR, from right side of head. Put up OLD WOMAN to left below TOWER. Move HAIR to left side, hanging down from window. Move OLD WOMAN to HAIR.
Rapunzel never saw anyone except the wicked old woman. As the years went by Rapunzel grew very lonely in her tower beside the deep, dark woods. Sometimes she sang to herself to keep from feeling so sad and lonely.	Take down OLD WOMAN. Take down HAIR.
One day a young prince was walking through the woods when he heard someone singing. Her voice was so beautiful and sounded so sad that he searched for the person who was singing. Finally, he came to the lonely tower. He knew there was someone inside the tower, but he could not find a door to enter. So he hid behind a rock to see what would happen.	Put up PRINCE to left of FOREST. Move PRINCE to left below TOWER. Move PRINCE to left below rock in FOREST.
Soon the wicked old woman came to the tower with food for Rapunzel. "Rapunzel, Rapunzel, let down thy hair," she called out. And the prince's eyes grew round with surprise as he saw the girl let down her long, long hair for the old woman to climb up.	Put up OLD WOMAN to left below TOWER. Put up HAIR (left side thereafter); move OLD WOMAN to HAIR.
The prince thought, "So that's how she enters the tower!" After the old woman had left, he stepped out from behind the rock and called, "Rapunzel, Rapunzel, let down thy hair," just as he had heard the old woman call.	Take down OLD WOMAN and HAIR. Move PRINCE to left of TOWER.
And just as before, the girl let down her long, long hair for the old woman to climb up. But imagine her surprise when she saw the young prince climb to the window. She had not seen any person except the old woman for many years.	Put up HAIR. Move PRINCE to HAIR. Move PRINCE to window on HAIR.

The young prince said, "Don't be afraid. I would never hurt you."

He asked Rapunzel how she came to be inside the lonely tower, and she told him about the wicked old woman. The prince felt very sorry for the lonely young girl, and he liked her very much. Every day he came to visit Rapunzel, and they became good friends.

Rapunzel and the prince decided to leave the tower and be married. Each time the prince came to visit, he brought a piece of rope. Rapunzel spent her time braiding all the ropes together to make one long enough for them to climb down from the tower someday. Soon she would be able to leave the lonely tower forever.

Put up coiled ROPE to right of RAPUNZEL's head.

Take down PRINCE.

Rapunzel was so happy about her secret plan that she could hardly think of anything else. One day when the old woman had just climbed up into the tower, Rapunzel said without thinking, "Why is it that you climb so slowly, when the young prince can climb up into the tower so fast and easy?"

Put up OLD WOMAN on HAIR, at window.

Then the old woman knew that Rapunzel had been having a secret visitor. The wicked woman searched the tower, and she found the hidden rope. She guessed the secret plan, and she made up an evil plan of her own. First she cut off all Rapunzel's beautiful long hair and left the hair in the tower. Then she tied the rope to the hook on the windowsill, and she and Rapunzel climbed down from the tower. The old woman took Rapunzel by the arm, and made her go far away into the forest, where she was lost and could not find her way out. Rapunzel had to wander alone in the dark forest.

> **Take down HAIR.**
>
> **Move ROPE to hook, hanging down. Move OLD WOMAN and RAPUNZEL to FOREST.**

When the old woman got back to the tower, she untied the rope and waited inside the tower. The young prince arrived, not knowing that anything had happened. He called out, "Rapunzel, Rapunzel, let down thy hair."

> **Move OLD WOMAN to behind TOWER, head in window. Take down ROPE. Put up PRINCE to left below TOWER.**

The old woman let down the long length of Rapunzel's hair, tied to the hook on the windowsill. When the prince reached the window, he saw the old woman there instead of Rapunzel. "What have you done? Where is she?" he cried.

> **Put up HAIR.**
> **Move PRINCE to HAIR.**

The old woman laughed and said, "You'll never find her again," as she pushed the prince off the tower. He fell hard into the bushes below. The thorns in the bushes scratched his eyes, so that he screamed and ran into the forest, unable to see.

> **Move PRINCE down, head against bush (near TOWER).**
>
> **Move PRINCE to FOREST.**

The prince wandered blindly in the woods for a long time. After awhile he thought he heard beautiful singing. He turned toward the sound, and he walked for a long, long way to try to find the source of the lovely music. The voice sounded like that of his beloved Rapunzel.

> **Take down TOWER and OLD WOMAN and HAIR.**

It was Rapunzel, singing in her loneliness and despair in the dark forest. Imagine her surprise when she saw her beloved prince coming toward her with his hands over his eyes, crying. Rapunzel ran to the prince, and she began to cry too. As her tears dropped onto his eyes, the scratches healed. He could see Rapunzel once again.

> **Move PRINCE to left of RAPUNZEL.**

Rapunzel and the prince found their way out of the forest together, and they went back to the prince's castle. There they were married, and they lived happily ever after.

> **Move PRINCE and RAPUNZEL to right of FOREST.**
>
> **Put up DISTANT CASTLE at right top.**

Follow-Up Activities

Questions for Discussion or Writing

1. During Rapunzel's years alone in the tower, what could she have done to pass the time? What did she think about? What did she see and hear through her window?

2. This story tells about a crime—Rapunzel's father stole some rampions from his neighbor's garden. If you were the neighbor and you caught someone stealing from your garden, what would you do? Why?

Craft

Braiding

Have children seated at tables with yarn, scissors, rulers, and masking tape. Read aloud and demonstrate a sample:

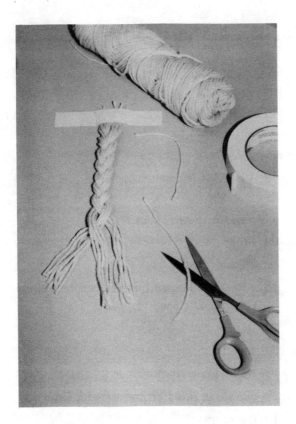

When Rapunzel was in the tower, the old woman and the prince climbed up her long braid of hair. You can make a braid of yarn like Rapunzel's braid of hair. Each of you needs to cut 21 lengths of yarn, each length at least 10 inches long. Divide the yarn into three bundles of seven strands each, and lay the strands side by side. Use masking tape to fasten the tops of all the strands to your table. First bring the left bundle over the center bundle, and place it in the center position. Then bring the right bundle over the center, and place it in the new center position. Repeat the procedure for the left bundle, then the right bundle, continuing until the entire piece is braided. Tie a string tightly around each end of the piece, and the braid will remain together.

Recommended Read-Aloud Books on Related Topics

Story about Hair

Davis, Biggs. *Katy's First Haircut.* Boston: Houghton Mifflin, 1985.

Stories about Princesses

Galdon, Paul. *Rumpelstiltskin.* New York: Clarion, 1985.

Lewison, Wendy Cheyette. *The Princess and the Potty.* New York: Simon & Schuster, 1994.

Yolen, Jane. *Sleeping Ugly.* New York: Coward, McCann & Geoghegan, 1981.

Books about Babies

Myers, Walter Dean. *Brown Angels: An Album of Pictures and Verse.* New York: HarperCollins, 1993.

Waber, Bernard. *Funny, Funny Lyle.* Boston: Houghton Mifflin, 1987.

The Frog Prince

Introduction

This story was collected and recorded by folklorists in Germany, Scotland, and England, with versions titled "The Frog King," "Iron Henry," and "The Well of the World's End." In addition to these stories, there are many other European folktales in which a man or woman, often of noble birth, is changed into a creature, such as a dragon or a frog, but can be changed back into human form by a kiss or some other show of love, acceptance, or loyalty. This flannelboard version of "The Frog Prince," like several others, shows the enchanted frog speaking entirely in rhyming verse.

Set-Up Instructions

Set up the following figures on the flannelboard:

    8. Water [spring], to right of center near top

71. Sun, top left corner

Set up figures on the table, left to right:

18, 18a. Man [prince character in this tale] with Crown

17. Woman [witch character]

28. Frog

  2. Distant Castle

15, 15b, 15c. Woman [princess character] with Crown and Cape

74. Ball

72. Moon

  9. Rich House (interior view)

20, 20a. Man [king character] with Crown

10. Bedroom

Read Aloud

<table>
<tr><td>——————— SCRIPT ———————</td><td>—— FLANNELBOARD ——</td></tr>
</table>

SCRIPT	FLANNELBOARD
One day a young, handsome prince was looking at his reflection in a deep spring of water. He did not hear a wicked old witch walk up quietly behind him, until she shrieked, "So you think you are handsome, do you? I'll make you handsome, indeed." And she cast a spell on the poor prince, turning him into a frog. He called out, "Oh, woe is me, woe is me! Will I a frog forever be?"	**Put up PRINCE to left above SPRING. Put up WITCH to left of PRINCE.**
The witch laughed, "Oh, no. All you have to do to break the spell is to stay close by the side of a beautiful lady for three days and three nights. That should be an easy task for such a handsome, green, slimy fellow as yourself!"	**Take down PRINCE; put up FROG.**
As the witch walked away laughing wickedly, the frog slipped quietly into the water and swam away by himself.	**Take down WITCH. Move FROG to right in SPRING.**
Close by the spring of water where the frog was living was a lovely, ancient castle where a king lived with his beautiful daughter. The young princess loved to play near the spring, throwing her golden ball high into the air and catching it as it came back down. She threw the ball high and caught it in her hand. She threw the ball even higher, and it landed at the edge of the spring, then it rolled into the water and sank slowly out of sight.	**Put up DISTANT CASTLE, top left.** **Put up PRINCESS just above SPRING. Put up BALL above PRINCESS.** **Move BALL to SPRING.**
The princess shouted and cried. Suddenly a voice very nearby said, "Who is that crying? Why did you shout? I shall be trying to help you out."	
The princess looked all around her, but she did not see anyone. She began to cry again, and the voice asked again, "Who is that crying? Why did you shout? I shall be trying to help you out."	
The voice sounded as though it came from the spring of water. The princess looked down, and there at the edge of the spring sat a frog. The frog opened his mouth and said, "Tell me, lady, tell me true, tell me what is wrong with you."	**Put up FROG to right of PRINCESS.**
The princess answered, "My favorite golden ball has fallen into the spring, and the water is so deep that I will never get it out."	
The frog said, "I'll bring the ball right back to you, if you will promise to be true, and let me come and live with you. I'll eat from your plate, and sit in your chair, and sleep beside your golden hair."	

SCRIPT	FLANNELBOARD

The princess answered, "Oh, yes, I'll give you anything, if you will just get back my golden ball."

Immediately the frog dived down into the water, and he swam back to the princess carrying the golden ball. She grabbed the ball and ran happily back into the castle.

Move FROG to BALL; move FROG and BALL to PRINCESS's feet.

Take down PRINCESS and BALL.

The frog called out after her, "Slow down! You run much faster than I. Or was your promise just a lie?"

But the princess did not slow down. She ran into the castle and slammed the door. The poor frog was left all alone at the spring.

Take down SUN; put up MOON.

That night inside the castle the princess was eating supper with her father, the king. She had not thought even once about what had happened that day at the spring, until she heard a sound like little footsteps at the door. The king said, "Go and see who is standing outside the door."

Take down FROG and DISTANT CASTLE. Put up RICH HOUSE (interior view) in top center. Put up PRINCESS in left chair, KING in right chair.

When the princess saw that it was the frog, she closed the door and came quickly back to the table. Her father asked, "What is wrong? Who is there?" When the princess told her father what had happened, he said, "You made a promise, and you must keep it. Bring the frog inside, and set him in your chair as you promised."

Put up FROG left of door.

The princess did not want to do this, but she opened the door as her father ordered. The frog jumped up to the table and began to eat from her plate. The princess decided that she didn't want any more to eat. Then the frog said, "I ate from your plate, and I sat in your chair. Now I want to sleep beside your hair."

Move PRINCESS to left. Move FROG to chair.

The princess said, "Oh, no!"

But her father reminded her, "You made a promise, and the frog did as he said he would. Now you must do as you said, also."

So very slowly the princess carried the frog to her bedroom, and she put him on her bed. She slept all night with the green frog on her pillow.

Put up BEDROOM in bottom center. Move FROG to pillow, then PRINCESS to bed.

The next two days the frog again sat right beside the princess at the table, and he ate food from her plate. He stayed right by her side all day long for two whole days.

Take down MOON; put up SUN. Move FROG and PRINCESS to table.

Each night the frog slept on the pillow right beside the princess's head all night long. The princess didn't think she could stand this for much longer.

On the third day, early in the morning, the princess awoke to find that the frog was not on her pillow. She jumped out of bed. Standing beside her was a handsome prince. She didn't know where he came from until he said, "I ate from your plate, and I sat in your chair, and I slept beside your golden hair. Three days and nights is what it would take, the evil witch's spell to break. And now, will you send me away, or may I stay?"

The princess smiled at the handsome young prince, for she was thinking that someday they could be married and live happily ever after.

Take down SUN; put up MOON. Move FROG and PRINCESS to bed.

Take down MOON; put up SUN. Take down FROG. Move PRINCESS to below bed, standing.

Put up PRINCE to left of PRINCESS.

Follow-Up Activities

Questions for Discussion or Writing

1. Have you ever made a promise that was very hard to keep? Why did you break your promise or keep it?

2. Why do you think the witch changed the prince into a frog? How was she feeling then? How did the prince feel before and after the change?

Activity

Making a Poster

Give each student old magazines, scissors, glue, a felt-tip marker, and a large piece of paper. Read aloud:

The princess felt many different emotions during this story. How did she feel when she lost her favorite ball? When the frog offered to help her? When the frog knocked at the door? When he turned into a prince? Find pictures of people in these magazines, and cut out the heads. Glue them onto a large piece of paper. Label each picture to tell how that person feels—happy, sad, scared, worried, etc.

Recommended Read-Aloud Books on Related Topics

Books about Frogs

Freschet, Berniece. *The Old Bullfrog.* New York: Scribner, 1968.

Kent, Jack. *The Caterpillar and the Polliwog.* Englewood Cliffs, N.J.: Prentice-Hall, 1982.

Langstaff, John. *Frog Went A-Courtin'.* San Diego: Harcourt, 1955, 1991.

Tresselt, Alvin. *The Frog in the Well.* New York: Lothrop, Lee & Shepard, 1958.

Wiesner, David. *Tuesday.* New York: Clarion, 1991.

The Fisherman and His Wife

Introduction

This folktale was collected from places widely separated on the globe. A Japanese folktale has a virtually identical plot. The Brothers Grimm recorded it in Germany, and it was published as "The Golden Fish" in *Old Peter's Russian Tales*. All the versions feature a somber mood and an emotionally wrenching ending.

Although this flannelboard version has been shortened and simplified, it is still a complicated story to present and requires a great deal of rehearsal before presentation. The felt figure of the castle covers the entire flannelboard. Because the castle must stay folded on the table until needed, it requires extra maneuvering for placement. Therefore, practice reading the appropriate sentences, setting down the text on the table, unfolding the felt figure and attaching it to the flannelboard, and picking up the text to resume reading so this presentation flows continuously. The tale provides a visual showcase for the most impressive felt figures, building in grandeur from the first humble cottage to the enormous castle. After this buildup, the sudden return to an empty beach setting makes a powerful impact on the audience.

Set-Up Instructions

Set up the flannelboard vertically with the following figures:

    8. Water [sea], against left edge below center

  71. Sun, top right corner

Set up figures on the table, left to right:

  20. Man [fisherman character in this tale]

  77. Net

  44. Fish

  17. Woman [wife character]

  72. Moon

 20a. Crown

 15c. Cape

Set up the following figures in a stack on the right end of the table, bottom to top:

  1. Castle (loosely folded)

 10. Bedroom

  9. Rich House (exterior view)

  7. Cottage (exterior view)

Read Aloud

<table>
<tr><th>SCRIPT</th><th>FLANNELBOARD</th></tr>
<tr><td>

Once upon a time beside the sea, there lived a fisherman. Although he worked very hard every day catching fish, he was very poor. He and his wife did not have a house. They lived on the beach beside the sea.

One day the fisherman caught a strange fish in his net. It fought and charged and pulled all day long, until the sun went down and the moon and stars came out. Finally the fisherman pulled the fish up out of the water.

The fish spoke to the man, "Do not take me out of the water. Do not kill me," it said, "for I am not what I seem, a fish. I am really an enchanted prince."

The fisherman put the fish back into the water. He said, "I would never have killed a talking fish, even if you were not an enchanted prince."

The night was calm and bright as the man went back to his wife without a fish. The fisherman told his wife about the strange thing that had happened.

She asked, "Did you set the fish free without even asking him to grant you a wish? For sparing his life, he would have been glad to give you anything you wanted."

The fisherman asked her, "But what do I want?"

She told him, "A house, a little house for us! In the morning, first thing, you must go back to the sea and ask the enchanted fish to give us a little house."

The wind came up a little in the night and woke up the fisherman at the first break of day. He walked to the edge of the sea and called, "Oh, enchanted prince, my wife wills much, but not as I will does she."

The magic fish appeared in the water and said, "What wills she?"

The fisherman replied, "She wills a little house, close by the side of the sea."

The fish answered, "Go on back; what she wills shall already be."

</td><td>

Put up FISHERMAN to left above SEA. Put up NET in FISHERMAN's hand. Put up WIFE to right below SEA.

Move NET end down to SEA. Put up FISH in NET.
Take down SUN; put up MOON.
Move NET and FISH up.

Move FISH to SEA. Take down NET.

Move FISHERMAN to left of WIFE.

Take down MOON; put up SUN. Move FISHERMAN to left above SEA.

Move FISH up in SEA.

Move FISH down in SEA.

</td></tr>
</table>

SCRIPT	**FLANNELBOARD**
When the fisherman walked back along the beach, he saw his wife standing outside a lovely little cottage. Together they spent the day exploring the outside and the inside of their new home. Inside there were chairs, a table, a rug, and a bed, and a fireplace with dishes, and a lamp, and all the things they would need to live in a humble cottage by the side of the sea.	**Put up COTTAGE (exterior view) at center top. Move FISHERMAN and WIFE to left of COTTAGE.** **Flip over COTTAGE.**
That night, the wind blew strongly, and the dark clouds rolled across the sky, keeping the fisherman and his wife awake. He said, "Are you happy now?"	**Take down SUN; put up MOON.**
She answered, "Why should we be happy with a little cottage, when the enchanted prince could have given us a lovely rich house? In the morning, you must go back and ask the magic fish for a bigger and richer house."	
At first light the next morning, the fisherman went down to the edge of the sea, and he called, "Oh, enchanted prince, my wife wills much, but not as I will does she."	**Take down MOON; put up SUN. Move FISHERMAN to left above SEA.**
The magic fish appeared in the water and said, "What wills she?"	**Move FISH up.**
The fisherman replied, "She wills a bigger house, richer than the cottage."	
The fish answered, "Go on back, what she wills shall already be."	**Move FISH down.**
When the fisherman returned to his wife's side, he saw her standing outside a lovely rich house. They spent the day exploring together inside their new home. They saw the windows with rich draperies, and the beautiful furniture in the dining room with a table and elegant chairs and food already on the table for them to eat. In the bedroom they saw more beautiful furniture, with lovely linens and cushions and even candles already lit for the night. During the night the wind howled all around the house, and the waves lapped strongly against the shore. The fisherman asked his wife, "Are you happy now?"	**Move FISHERMAN back to left of WIFE. Take down COTTAGE; put up RICH HOUSE (exterior view). Flip over RICH HOUSE.** **Take down RICH HOUSE; put up BEDROOM.** **Take down SUN; put up MOON.**
She answered, "Why should we be happy in a house? It is just a house. We could just as easily have had a castle. Tomorrow you must go back, and you must ask for a castle."	

SCRIPT	FLANNELBOARD
So early the next morning the fisherman walked to the edge of the sea, and he called, "Oh, enchanted prince, my wife wills much, but not as I will does she."	**Take down MOON; put up SUN. Move FISHERMAN to left above SEA.**
The magic fish appeared again in the water and said, "What wills she?"	**Move FISH up.**
The fisherman replied, "She wills a castle."	
The fish answered, "Go on back; what she wills shall already be."	
The fisherman walked back toward the spot where he had left his wife. But before he got very far he saw an enormous castle, with towers and turrets and flags waving, right at the water's edge. The fisherman looked around for his wife, and he saw her standing to the side of their new home. He asked her, "Surely you are happy now?"	**Take down everything. Put up CASTLE.** **Put up FISHERMAN to right below CASTLE, WIFE to his left.**
She answered, "Why should I live in a castle as the wife of a fisherman? I should be queen. Go back now and tell the magic fish."	
So the fisherman walked back toward the sea, and he called, "Oh, enchanted prince, my wife wills much, but not as I will does she."	**Move FISHERMAN to left above CASTLE.**
The magic fish appeared, and said, "What wills she?"	**Put up FISH in CASTLE water.**
The fisherman replied, "She wills to be queen."	
The fish answered, "Go on back; what she wills shall already be."	**Move FISH down in CASTLE water.**
When the man walked back to his wife, he saw that she wore the crown and cape of a queen. He asked, "Are you happy now?"	**Move FISHERMAN to right of WIFE. Put up CROWN and CAPE on her.**
She replied, "We shall see." By then the moon was beginning to rise above the horizon. The woman saw it and said, "I am queen. I should command everyone and everything. Go back, and tell the fish that I must command the sun, the moon, and the stars."	**Put up MOON to right of CASTLE.**
Just then a terrible storm came up. The wind whipped huge, dark clouds through the sky, covering all the stars and the moon, and plunging the world into darkness.	**Take down MOON.**

The Fisherman and His Wife **157**

—————— **SCRIPT** ——————	⋮	—— **FLANNELBOARD** ——

Frightened, the fisherman ran back to the edge of the sea. He called loudly over the roar of the sea and the storm, "Oh, enchanted prince, my wife wills much, but not as I will does she."

Move FISHERMAN to left above CASTLE water.

The magic fish appeared in the water and said, "What wills she?"

Move FISH up.

The fisherman replied, "To command the sun, and the moon, and the stars."

Angrily the fish answered, "Go on back; all is as it was before."

Take down everything except FISHERMAN.

Suddenly the storm stopped. The wind died down, and the clouds parted, and the moon and the stars shone out. Once again the fisherman walked by the side of the sea. As far as he and his wife could walk there was nothing at all along the beach beside the sea.

Put up MOON at top right. Put up SEA at bottom left. Put up WIFE to right of FISHERMAN.

Follow-Up Activities

Questions for Discussion or Writing

1. Have you ever wished for something, and then received it? What was it? Did you like it after you got it? Why or why not?

2. If the magic fish would grant your wishes, what would you wish for? What would you ask the fish to grant you for yourself? For someone you know? For the whole world?

Game

Fish, Net, or Water

This is a variation of the Japanese game called "Scissors, Paper, Stone." Pairs of players stand facing each other, each person with one hand behind the back. Together they chant, "Magic fish, grant my wish." On the word "wish" each player brings out his or her hand in either the fish (hand open flat), the net (hand cupped), or the water (closed fist) position. The net conquers the fish, the fish conquers the water, and the water conquers the net. Players keep repeating the chant and the contest.

Recommended Read-Aloud Books on Related Topics

Stories about Situations That Got Out of Control

Asch, Frank. *Popcorn: A Frank Asch Bear Story.* New York: Parent's, 1979.

Coombs, Patricia. *The Magic Pot.* New York: Lothrop, Lee & Shepard, 1977.

Krakauer, Hong Yee Lee. *Rabbit Mooncakes.* Boston: Little, Brown, 1994. (includes Cantonese vocabulary list)

Van Allsburg, Chris. *Two Bad Ants.* Boston: Houghton Mifflin, 1988.

Viorst, Judith. *Alexander and the Terrible, Horrible, No Good, Very Bad Day.* New York: Atheneum, 1972.

The Three Sillies

Introduction

Andrew Lang collected and published folktales from many different places at the end of the nineteenth century and beginning of the twentieth. One story in his collection was the tale sometimes called "The Six Sillies" and sometimes called "The Three Sillies." Stories about silly people who succeed in spite of, or even because of, their silliness are called "noodlehead tales." Just as in other noodlehead tales, this story's mood is light, and everybody lives happily ever after. The story is fun for the audience because even young children can delight in being smarter than the noodleheads.

Set-Up Instructions

Set up the following figures on the flannelboard:

    7. Cottage (interior view), near center top

   71. Sun, top right

Set up figures on the table, left to right:

   14. Woman [Else character in this tale]

   16. Woman [mother character]

   20. Man [father character]

   19. Man [Hans character]

   78. Jug

   66. Barrel

   76. Hatchet

   17. Woman [old woman character]

   27. Cow

   52. Hay

   65. Rope (coiled loosely)

   72. Moon

   10. Bedroom

   18, 18b. Man [young man character] with Trousers

    8. Water (folded loosely) [pond]

   53. Rake

   15. Woman [young woman character]

Read Aloud

SCRIPT	FLANNELBOARD
Once upon a time there lived a girl named Else, who had a great deal of imagination. She was always thinking of new ideas and fantastic stories. Her mother and father thought she was very clever.	**Put up ELSE to right of COTTAGE.** **Put up MOTHER and FATHER to right of ELSE.**
One day a young man knocked at the door. His name was Hans, and he was searching every town for a wife. Else's parents invited Hans to come in for a visit. As they all talked and visited, Hans mentioned that he was looking for a woman to marry, who was very clever—very, very clever. Else's father told him, "Oh, our Else is the cleverest woman you would ever find."	**Put up HANS to left of COTTAGE.** **Move HANS to chair.**
Her mother added, "The very cleverest!" Then she turned to Else and said, "Else, run down to the cellar for some of that wonderful cider you made, and bring a cup of cider back for Hans."	**Move ELSE to left below COTTAGE, with JUG in hand.**
So clever Else hurried down the stairs to the cellar. As she walked toward the cider barrel, she happened to look upward. There near the ceiling of the cellar someone had left a hatchet, stuck into the wall and forgotten.	**Put up BARREL to far left below COTTAGE.** **Put up HATCHET in center below COTTAGE.**
Else looked at that hatchet, and she began to imagine. "What if," she said, "what if I marry Hans, and we have a baby, and the baby grows bigger, and then he comes down to the cellar for some cider? If that hatchet falls, then the hatchet will hit our baby on the head, and he will surely die! Oh, our poor little baby!" Forgetting about the cider altogether, Else started to cry.	
After awhile, Else's mother began to wonder what was keeping Else so long down in the cellar, so she went downstairs to find out. She exclaimed, "Else! Why are you crying?"	**Move MOTHER to left of ELSE.**
And Else replied, "Oh, it is so sad! What if I marry Hans, and we have a baby, and the baby grows bigger, and then he comes down to the cellar for some cider? If that hatchet falls, then the hatchet will hit our baby on the head, and he will surely die! Oh, our poor little baby!" Forgetting about the cider altogether, Else and her mother started to cry.	
After awhile, Else's father began to wonder what was keeping Else and her mother so long down in the cellar, so he went downstairs to find out. He exclaimed, "Why are you two crying?"	**Move FATHER to left of MOTHER.**

And his wife replied, "Oh, it is so sad! What if Else marries Hans, and they have a baby, and the baby grows bigger, and then he comes down to the cellar for some cider? If that hatchet falls, then it will hit their baby on the head, and he will surely die!" Forgetting about the cider altogether, Else and her mother and her father started to cry.

After awhile, poor Hans began to wonder what was keeping everybody so long down in the cellar. He said to himself, "Maybe they are waiting for me to join them down there for a cup of cider. I'll go down to see." So he went downstairs to find out. He exclaimed, "Oh, why is everybody crying? What has happened?"

Move HANS to right of ELSE.

Then Else's father answered, "Oh, it is so sad! What if Else marries you, and you have a baby, and the baby grows bigger, and then he comes down to the cellar for some cider? If that hatchet falls, then the hatchet will hit your baby on the head, and he will surely die!" And they all cried even louder.

But Hans, instead of crying, began to laugh. He laughed and laughed until he fell down on the floor, and then he laughed some more. Finally, he stood up, wiped his eyes on the back of his hand, and pulled the hatchet out of the wall. He said, "There, Else, I believe that will take care of the problem. And now I really must be going."

Move HANS to lying position; move back to standing position. Take down HATCHET.

But Else's father called out, "Hans, wait! We need to talk about your marriage to clever Else."

Hans just laughed again, and he said as he was leaving the house, "The only way that I would marry *her* is if I should find three people with even sillier ideas than hers in the same day. I believe that *that* takes care of the problem now." And without another word, Hans left their cottage.

Move HANS to right of COTTAGE.

Take down BARREL, ELSE, MOTHER, FATHER.

He walked for a long time, until he came to another cottage. There a very strange sight met his eyes. A woman was pushing a cow up onto the roof. The cow did not want to go, but the woman forced the cow up onto the roof. Hans said, "Hello, there! What are you doing?"

Flip over COTTAGE to exterior view. Move HANS to far left side. Put up OLD WOMAN on left side of COTTAGE. Put up COW to right of chimney; put up HAY on roof.

The woman replied, "Can't you see my good idea? I'm putting the cow up on the thatched roof to eat the fresh-cut hay."

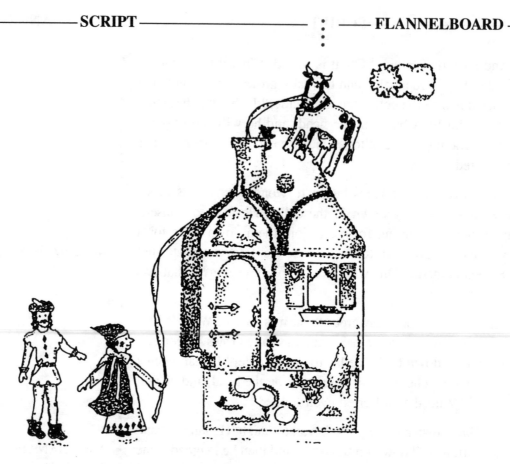

Hans asked very politely, "Wouldn't it be easier to throw the hay down onto the ground for the cow to eat?"

But the woman replied, "Oh, no, because I can keep the cow up on the roof by tying this rope that goes from her neck around the chimney, and onto my wrist. That way, if the cow moves, I'll know it."

Put up ROPE, from COW's neck to behind chimney, to OLD WOMAN's arm.

Before Hans could reply to that, the cow slipped down off the roof, and the rope pulled the woman up the wall and around the chimney, where she stuck fast.

Move COW and ROPE to right of COTTAGE; move OLD WOMAN to roof with head above chimney.

Hans walked on down the road. He walked for a long time, until the sun went down and the moon began to rise in the night sky. Hans saw an inn nearby, and he asked for a room for the night. There was no room available at the inn until another man said Hans could have his room because he was getting ready to leave.

Take down COTTAGE, HAY, OLD WOMAN, ROPE, COW. Take down SUN; put up MOON. Put up BEDROOM in center of board. Put up YOUNG MAN to left of BEDROOM.

Hans gratefully accepted so he would have a place to sleep for the night. But while he was waiting for the room he was very surprised to see the strange man jumping up and down, over and over, by the dresser. Hans asked him, "What are you doing?"

Move YOUNG MAN to above dresser. Put up TROUSERS on dresser.

The man answered, "I'm trying to jump into my trousers. Every day, it is so hard to get into them. Sometimes I land with one leg in my trousers and sometimes with the other leg in, but it takes me about an hour of jumping to get both legs in my trousers at the same time. How long does it take you to get dressed?"

Hans showed him how to step into his trousers, one leg at a time. The young man was very grateful to be able to get dressed so quickly. He left early that night.

Move YOUNG MAN down; move TROUSERS onto him. Take down YOUNG MAN.

Very early the next morning, as the moon was setting but before the sun was up, Hans began walking again, shaking his head sadly and muttering, "A man who tried to jump into his trousers, and a woman who was tied to her cow on the roof. Those are the two biggest sillies I've seen in my whole life, and all in one day! What next?"

Move MOON to center right. Take down BEDROOM.

Put up POND at right bottom. Move HANS to left of POND.

He found out just as the moon set out of sight behind a pond. A young woman was trying to rake something out of the water. She would rake very hard, and then she would look into the water and stamp her foot angrily. Then she would rake some more.

Take down MOON. Put up YOUNG WOMAN with RAKE just to left of POND.

Hans watched her for awhile, and then he asked, "Did you lose something in the water?"

"Yes," replied the woman angrily. Didn't you just see the moon fall into this pond? I'm trying to find it before it drowns. Just think—if I don't rescue the moon, it won't come up tomorrow night."

Hans walked on down the road, laughing to himself. "Thinking that the moon fell into the pond when it set! That's the third biggest silly I've ever seen, and all in one day!" Then Hans stopped in the middle of the road and thought awhile. He said, "Compared to these three sillies, Else seems very clever after all."

Take down YOUNG WOMAN, RAKE, and POND.

So he began to walk back toward Else's cottage again as fast as he could walk. By the time the sun had come up that morning, Hans was asking Else to marry him. And by the time she had said, "Oh yes," she was imagining all sorts of lovely things for the whole family.

Move HANS to far left. Put up SUN left top. Put up ELSE to right of HANS, hands touching.

Follow-Up Activities

Questions for Discussion or Writing

1. In the story the mother, father, and daughter were all afraid that someday a child might go into the cellar and be killed by a falling hatchet. Have you ever worried about things that might happen someday? Did you believe those things could really happen? Why or why not? What helps you to stop worrying?

2. At the end of the story the daughter was enjoying using her imagination to picture lovely things for her family in the future. What good things do you imagine for your life in the future? What things will be the same as now? What things will be different?

Activity

Group Storytelling

With the children sitting in a circle, read aloud:

> Do you have an active imagination like Else? You are going to create your own fairy tale. One of you will begin the story "Once upon a time there was . . . ," and say two sentences. Then another person will add the next two sentences to continue

the same story. Everyone must listen carefully and continue the story. When a person finishes talking, think quietly for a moment before you volunteer to add to the story.

Each time a child finishes speaking, wait quietly to encourage thinking before calling on someone to add the next sentences to the story. To encourage careful listening and thinking, discourage children from adding immediately to the story.

Recommended Read-Aloud Books on Related Topics

Stories about Silly Folks

Arnold, Ted. *No Jumping on the Bed.* New York: Dial, 1978.

Dunbar, Joyce. *Seven Sillies.* New York: Artists & Writers Guild, 1994.

Lionni, Leo. *An Extraordinary Egg.* New York: Knopf, 1994.

Marshall, James. *The Stupids Take Off.* Boston: Houghton Mifflin, 1989.

Rattigan, Jama Kim. *Truman's Aunt Farm.* Boston: Houghton Mifflin, 1994.

Selected Resources

Arbuthnot, May Hill, comp. *Time for Fairy Tales Old and New.* Glenview, Ill.: Scott, Foresman, 1961.

Arnott, Kathleen. *Animal Folk Tales Around the World.* New York: H. Z. Walck, 1971.

Courlander, Harold. *The Tiger's Whisker and Other Tales and Legends from Asia and the Pacific.* New York: Harcourt, 1959.

Crossley-Holland, Devin. *British Folk Tales: New Versions.* New York: Orchard, 1987.

Gág, Wanda, transl. *Tales from Grimm.* Eau Claire, Wis.: Hale, 1936.

Jacobs, Joseph. *English Fairy Tales.* New York: Schocken, 1967.

———. *More English Folks and Fairy Tales.* New York: Putnam, n.d.

Lang, Andrew. *The Blue Fairy Book.* Harmondsworth, Middlesex, Eng.: Kestrel, 1975.

Leach, Maria, ed. *Funk and Wagnall's Standard Dictionary of Folklore, Mythology and Legend.* New York: Funk & Wagnall's, 1972.

Mannheim, Ralph, transl. *Grimm's Tales for Young and Old: The Complete Stories.* Garden City, N.Y.: Doubleday, 1977.

Montgomerie, Norah. *To Read and to Tell.* London: The Bodley Head, 1962.

Morel, Eve, ed. *Fairy Tales and Fables.* New York: Grossett & Dunlap, 1970.

Opie, Iona, and Peter Opie. *The Classic Fairy Tales.* London: Oxford University Press, 1974.

Robinson, Gail, and Douglas Hill. *Coyote the Trickster: Legends of the North American Indians.* New York: Crane Russak, 1976.

Segal, Lore, and Randall Jarrell, transl., and Maurice Sendak, selector. *The Juniper Tree and Other Tales from Grimm.* New York: Farrar, Straus & Giroux, 1976.

Doris Hicks was a teacher and school librarian in public schools near Dallas, Texas, for many years. She used the flannelboard and hand puppets in her storytime presentations. The story follow-up activities in this book came from her experience in elementary school libraries and classrooms as well as public library programs for ages three to eleven.

Sandy Weber Mahaffey is a free-lance artist living in the country near Decatur, Texas, with her husband and two daughters. An active member of the Wise County Art Association, she works in all media, preferring pencil, ink, and watercolor. Mahaffey attended San Jacinto College in Pasadena, Texas, and the University of North Texas in Denton and graduated with art degrees from both. She has traveled to Europe, touring the castles, towns, and countryside. The illustrations in this book set out to capture some of that old world charm.